Did You Ever
Love Me?

THE MILLION COPY BESTSELLING
AUTHOR

TONI MAGUIRE

WITH CASSIE COOK

Did You Ever Love Me?

Abused by the ones who were supposed to keep her safe

EBURY
PRESS

3 5 7 9 10 8 6 4 2

Ebury Press, an imprint of Ebury Publishing
20 Vauxhall Bridge Road
London SW1V 2SA

Ebury Press is part of the Penguin Random House group of companies
whose addresses can be found at global.penguinrandomhouse.com

Penguin
Random House
UK

First published by Ebury Press in 2018

www.penguin.co.uk

A CIP catalogue record for this book is available from the British Library

ISBN 9781785037665

Typeset in 11.25/16.5 pt Adobe Garamond Pro
by Integra Software Services Pvt. Ltd, Pondicherry

Printed and bound in Great Britain by Clays Ltd, Elcograf S.p.A.

MIX
Paper from
responsible sources
FSC
www.fsc.org   FSC® C018179

Penguin Random House is committed to a
sustainable future for our business, our readers
and our planet. This book is made from Forest
Stewardship Council® certified paper.

I dedicate this book to all survivors — you are not alone, there is a light.

Contents

Prologue

Why, so many people ask, why don't children talk?

I could tell them by asking that question they must never have felt fear. Not the fear of a bad school report, or of not having the right dress to wear to a party, nor being late for an appointment. No, not that one; but the other, the one that sits heavily on our chests while we sleep, creeps into our dreams and slides down our throats, choking back any words asking for help that might have been on the tips of our tongues.

No, that emotion has never been their constant companion. For if it had, they would know that once held in its grip, we are in a place without mercy, where both reason and logical thinking cease to exist.

Ask the person with claustrophobia why they cannot enter a lift. Or the one with agoraphobia why their legs shake and their feet will not move to take them outside. They have very few answers because they understand their behaviour is irrational. But those demons that cause chests to tighten and breathing to become pants of terror pay scant attention to reason.

I grew up in the dark age of ignorance, two decades before organisations like Childline told us that just one phone call could make us safe. When I was a small child the thought of telling anyone in authority the truth simply did not enter my mind, or the minds of those who, like me, suffered in silence. We had no faith in adults, no trust whatsoever. For we were the awkward children, the grubby ones, the ones who stood alone in the playground, the ones whose homework was ill-done, the ones who were difficult to love. We seldom received a kind word from an authoritative figure, nor did we expect to. For we were all too aware it was us who were blamed for our parents' neglect.

The well-watered seeds of suspicion, planted by those in charge, gradually became so firmly embedded in our minds that it was impossible to speak out – to tell where those bruises came from, or that we often went to bed hungry. When our bad marks for class work were ridiculed and we heard the sniggers of our peers, we could not say that fear peppered our sleep with nightmares and deadened our concentration.

Was it likely then that we could have stood up and said 'Please, Miss, my mum and dad came home from the pub drunk and their rowing all night stopped me from sleeping' or 'Please, Miss, my dad spent my mum's housekeeping money at the dogs and there was no breakfast this morning. And those bruises on my legs ... Well, Miss, my dad took his belt to me when I told him I had to finish my homework. And my broken arm last year when I said I fell out of a tree ... that was my dad too. That's why my homework never gets done.'

Those were never going to be sentences that the children of abuse could utter.

If we could not tell our teachers that, then how could we, with eyes cast down and cheeks stained red, whisper the words describing the very worst?

That we did not like the way Daddy crept into our rooms and touched us in the places we thought were private?

There was a time, just once, when I summoned up my courage and tried to ask for help. But that was a sad mistake, one I can still hardly bear to think about. For when I tried to tell, I had clearly said the unsayable. Instead of receiving help it was disdainful looks and harsh words that were thrown at me.

Because of the repercussions that followed that one time when I put my trust in an adult, I never tried again. For after that hadn't I been told what would happen, should I talk? Like tiny drops of poison entering my bloodstream so my parents' whispered threats entered my mind, spiking it with anxiety and distrust.

No one will believe you.

They will say you are a dirty little girl making up those stories; something I had already learnt to be true.

When I entered my teens and thought my voice might be believed it was shame that silenced me. But not before I had tackled my father, who on hearing my threats mocked me.

Wasn't I the one who had taken part in those sordid deeds? he asked, a glimmer of malevolence in his eyes.

The one who had kept quiet all those years?

Who would believe I hadn't enjoyed it?

'Nobody will love you if you talk, Cassie,' he said. 'You will be the one shunned. You will lose everything.'

And because I believed him, this prophesy eventually came true.

It was only later, when it was too late, that I realised maybe another life might have been possible.

And when those memories slide into my head they bring with them a question I need answered. It is the one that angers me still. Why? Why did no one ask?

All those teachers and those heads of schools that worked during the fifties, sixties, seventies and eighties, they saw the bruises, the neglect, the nervousness. Why did they never ask?

I remember looking at those adults – 'See me,' I prayed, 'see what is happening to me.

'Can't you look at me? Why don't you ask me?

'I could tell if you did.'

But no one heard my silent pleas.

No one rescued me.

Chapter One

I am no longer young. But then neither am I lonely or unloved. Not now, not any more.

I love my job, working with the elderly. This is where they come to when they need the extra care that those outside can no longer give. This place is called a home. I like that word for that is what we all try and make it. When I step through the doors to begin my shift I feel it is also my home and those elderly people who are spending their last days there, they are now my family. My arm goes easily around thin shoulders to give a slight hug and each time I hold the hand of a resident I am moved by the weightless papery feel of it resting in mine. I grieve when someone in my care slips away. Sometimes it is one who remains sprightly to the end so that I am unprepared for their death and that intensifies the pain I feel. I go to the funeral and my body shakes with silent sobs. All too often it is just us – the carers and a few of the residents – who attend, for only faded photographs remain of lifelong friends and the spouses they have outlived. Daughters and sons have moved to faraway places – Australia, America – but sometimes, even more sadly, only a county away.

It's very hard not to have favourites although I have been warned to keep an emotional distance, something I cannot always bring myself to do. There are always those who pull on my heartstrings. I feel the bond between us the moment they arrive and, as our eyes meet, I know they feel the same.

There is Doris with her beautiful hands. Young hands still, though her face bears the wrinkles that time has bestowed on her. She was once a famous concert pianist. Travelled the world, she tells me. She delights in drawing back the curtain separating the past from the present to show me the world she once inhabited.

'There were lovers,' she says, punctuated by her still-girlish laugh, 'but only one husband. He did not last long.'

'Oh, he was a decent man,' she adds archly, 'he fell in love with my playing. He told me that almost the first time he took me out.'

Her cheeks take on the flush of youth each time she shares her stories with me. Names of composers that I have never heard of trip off her tongue, as do the names of the concert halls. I can almost hear the sound of the applause and see the size and colours of the many bouquets.

I venture to ask questions.

What happened to her husband is one such enquiry.

The answers vary depending on her mood but some are consistent.

'It was not long after the war finished when we met,' she tells me. 'He was not one of those who waited at the stage door with flowers in their hands and hope on their faces. He had a friend who knew the manager of the concert hall I was playing in. A dinner was arranged. Such a shortage of young men then, so of course I was flattered to be singled out. But once that ring was on my finger he wanted me to play only for him. No more travelling, no more concerts ... Stay at home and have children.'

'What did you do?' I always ask Doris.

'I left.'

But she does not volunteer any more information on that subject, which leaves my curiosity unsatisfied.

Another old lady, Dorothy, remembers the days when she was a child more than she does anything from the present. It is the war years she wants to reminisce about.

She tells me about the bombs that fell over London and the nights she had spent in the crowded Underground bomb shelters.

'Most of the children were sent away then,' she says. 'It was terrible for those who lost their parents and had no home to come back to when it was all over.'

I never ask if she was one of those. Instead I turn her away from recounting more sad tales by swapping some of mine for hers, for as well as listening, I am encouraged to share experiences of what is happening outside the home and in my own life.

That time of the afternoon, when tea is served and ginger biscuits are dunked into the hot milky liquid, inquisitive eyes turn to me, waiting for answers to their questions. With my own cup balanced precariously on my knee I tell them of the era I grew up in, the late sixties and the seventies.

I recount how we were not a rich family, but a happy one. I draw pictures with words of a plump, loving mother, reading my brothers and me bedtime stories, before tucking us in at night. I try and put life into my descriptions of the park where we were taken to feed the ducks and the thrill of excitement every time my father, his liquorice dark eyes sparkling with good humour, and with head thrown back, pushed my swing higher and higher until all I could see was the sky.

I talk about my happy school days, how I loved drawing and writing poetry and when I presented my paintings to my mother I had been so proud when she pinned and taped them to the kitchen walls. How I squirmed with delight when she heaped praise on every single one of my early attempts. Crayoned drawings full of blue, red and green squiggles which I said were people, but they were nearly as tall as the little square houses I drew over and over.

Some afternoons I take my elderly audience straight back to my teenage years – the dances, the boyfriends, my first job, the fun I had and the fashionable clothes I wore then.

But of course none of what I tell them is true. Neither my childhood nor my teenage years had been anything like that.

Chapter Two

I was still a young woman when I first had therapy. It was not my decision; that was made for me. I was given a card, thick cream paper with a name printed on the front. Flipping it over, I saw the address and time of the appointment written in neat, cursive letters. On reading it, I said that yes, I knew where it was and which bus would take me there.

I placed the card in my pocket with my fingers still curled around its smoothness and made my way home. Much as I would have liked to have taken that small oblong card out, torn it up, scattered the pieces and let them disappear into the air, I understood my choices had come to an end. There would be consequences if I did not attend and those I was loath to face.

Two days later, at 10am, I caught the bus that took me from the council estate I had hardly left for several months along roads where developments of well-cared-for private houses sprawled on either side. Neat semi-detached red brick squares with white net curtains at the windows and clipped box hedges dividing the gardens from their neighbours'. Seeing them, my mind floated back to what seemed a lifetime ago, when I was a child. I had watched those houses springing up like wild flowers until our estate, with its rundown houses, seemed like a forlorn island lost in the midst of their elegance. The area the council had designated for us was one reserved for problem families. Which, it appeared to be, that anyone with more than two children was classed as. Certainly there was some truth in it for unkempt gardens, grubby curtains, overflowing dustbins and streets constantly littered with unidentifiable debris were the norm there.

It was the general consensus that children from the streets where I grew up were badly disciplined, ran wild and once grown, would be nothing but trouble to their families and society while those who lived on the private estates had other ambitions for their offspring.

The architecture of the private houses, with their through lounges, two-and-a-half bedrooms and patches of manicured lawns, might not have been much different from ours, but they were still a different world. At weekends lawns were mowed, shiny Austin Morrises and Cortinas washed and polished, and children's playtime was supervised. Those who lived there were proud to be homeowners, not tenants, as many of their parents still were.

Our section of the town was an eyesore, one they resented being in their midst. They did not want us there any more than my mother wanted me, or for that matter my two brothers. I had watched those carefree first-time buyers drive up to their new homes. I'd witnessed the delivery trucks arrive and furniture, often still in its plastic covering, being carried in. Now those same young couples are elderly, their offspring grown and already moved away.

Most of their children attended the same school as me. I remember those groups of well-dressed girls who had already formed their own little cliques well before their schooldays had begun. Most probably they had known each other ever since their mothers pushed their prams side by side. They would have been in the same mother and baby groups before being enrolled in play school and by the time infanthood was left behind, they were already attending each other's birthday parties. I might understand now why they all stayed together in little groups, but then I just felt like an outcast.

The cold shoulder treatment seemed to be learnt at a very young age. I cringed every time a small child, who could have played the part of an angel in a nativity play, showed obvious reluctance to sit next to me in class. I tried to make myself invisible when envelopes containing invitations to birthday parties were passed around. At five I thought one was going to be for me, my hand already raised to take it and my mouth beginning to stretch into a delighted smile, when it was given to a little girl seated just behind me. By the time I was six I accepted that not one of those invitations was ever going to be placed in my hand. Even now, all those years later, the hurt I have repeatedly told myself is buried rears its head from out of its hiding place and bites sharply when I least expect to feel its fangs.

As a child I had not understood why those self-assured small children, with their pressed clothes and shiny hair, were told to keep away from us. With my older brother, I thought it was just because he was different. I was aware that he was always alone in the playground. I also knew he was mocked and tormented. Hadn't I seen boys mimicking his peculiar walk and imitating his slow speech? It made me uneasy. I wanted a teacher to stop it, to tell those boys to leave him alone – they must have seen it happening. But nothing was ever done.

No sooner had I moved out of the infant class than being ignored in the playground also became my fate, as it was for my little brother a couple of years later.

As the bus turned a corner, I blinked and told those thoughts to disappear. There were more important issues I had to deal with. 'Get a grip, Cassie,' I told myself, 'stop dwelling on the past. Never does any good, does it?' Then, glancing through the window of the bus, I saw the pale green leaves of the plane trees were unfurling. Spring was finally making its appearance. Maybe, I thought, the signs of a new year beginning also heralded a fresh start for me.

The next stop was mine. It was only a walk of a few hundred yards from where I alighted to the address on the card.

Was I nervous that day? I think I was past that, my feelings already deadened by the events of the few weeks prior to it.

I rang the bell next to the nameplate on the door and a disembodied voice asked for my name before bidding me to enter. Once inside I was informed that Ms Travis would see me in just a few moments and to take a seat. There were several chairs but a gangling dark-haired youth was the only person occupying one. Behind them was a large, ornate gilded mirror. I gave it an involuntary glance and saw looking back at me a rather shabby woman fast approaching middle age, whose too-tight skirt was rucked at the hips and the buttons on her blouse, bought in a charity shop, were straining to keep closed. Her light brown hair was badly in need of styling and worry had placed deep creases onto her forehead, while her unmade-up face, puffy through lack of sleep, was pale and drawn.

'That is me,' I thought, feeling a wave of depression. Where had the person I was disappeared to? For the woman in the mirror was almost a stranger.

I longed for a cigarette and my hand went instinctively into my bag before I spotted the no-smoking sign. My fingers twitched with the need to hold one, a few drags would calm me. I thought of going outside, just a minute would be all it would take to ease that nicotine craving. But then I might be late for my appointment and that would not look good, would it? 'Cassie,' my inner voice said unsympathetically, 'where's your willpower gone? You can go without one for an hour, can't you?' 'Of course I can,' I said firmly to that hectoring voice, lowering myself onto one of the chairs. I picked up a magazine and unseeingly flicked through it.

A few moments later I was ushered into a room bearing little resemblance to any doctor's surgery I had visited before. There was a desk with a computer sitting on it but apart from that, with its comfy chairs and light oak coffee table, it had more the appearance of a sitting room than a surgery.

The woman who greeted me with a warm friendly smile was also unexpected. In her early thirties, she was dressed casually in snug-fitting jeans and a crisp white shirt. Short blonde hair was neatly tucked behind her ears and I noticed her unlined face and warm brown eyes.

'Cassie, come in,' she said, as though I was a welcome guest dropping in for a coffee. 'Make yourself comfortable,' and she eased herself into the chair with its back to the window and beckoned me to sit opposite her.

'Cassie,' she explained, 'today we are just going to get to know each other. So tell me a little about yourself and how you think I can help you.'

What did she expect me to say, I wondered, feeling panicky. I wanted to tell her my being there was all a mistake and I could manage without her help. But that was not the message I managed to convey, for no sooner did I open my mouth to speak than my voice choked up with barely suppressed tears.

Without any comment she passed me a box of tissues. She was clearly used to distraught patients, I thought, and it was then that I realised that was exactly what I was: a distraught patient. With a wad of tissues clenched in my fist, my throat still so dry words were sticking to it, I managed to splutter out some details of my marriage. How he had left, but not why, not that first time. It was still too raw, too painful, for me to tell her.

14

CHAPTER TWO

My children were another subject I wanted to stay away from. I had noticed a wedding ring on her finger. Was she a mother? I wondered, but dare not ask. For if she was, therapist or not, she might blame me for what had happened to them. Certainly everyone else did. Neighbours I once felt were friends now averted their gaze whenever they saw me. My mother-in-law, who I had once been so close to, refused to speak to me, while my last remaining friend, the one that comes in liquid form, had finally betrayed me. No longer did it dim my memories for they were there from the moment I awoke until night came and fitful sleep grudgingly took hold. Not in a soft embrace, no, it is never that, but to a dark place where beneath my flickering lids the images whirling around my head both mock and taunt me.

Now, facing this woman who, I had been told, was not there to judge me but to help, I found it increasingly difficult to offer more than a few morsels of information. Each time I stopped she waited patiently for me to continue. The only question she asked after a long period of muteness was if I needed some water to which I shook my head.

Each time my words dried up the silence between us was oppressive. I wanted to give her some facts that might just make her see me in a better light, but after nearly half my time had been used up, they remained unspoken.

'Cassie,' and with this she leant slightly forward, then, 'you do understand why you are here?'

'Yes,' I replied, knowing full well it was a question she already knew the answer to. She might not have had a file full of notes about me sitting between us, but they were, I was sure, on her computer and had been read thoroughly.

'Well, let's talk about that a little, shall we?' And then 'No,' as though reading my mind, 'not the facts I have been given, they only tell me what finally happened. It's the why they happened we have to look at. That is the reason you are here.

'So shall we start at the beginning?'

'How far back do you want me to go?' I wondered.

And again she answered my voiceless question.

'Let's start with your earliest memories, shall we?'

As she spoke her words acted like a key turning in a rusty lock and slowly the door leading to my childhood began to creak open. Behind it lay the grim corridor leading to a place I did not wish to visit. I could feel my heart hammering inside my ribcage, my breath was turning into pants and I fought down the panic that stops enough air getting into my lungs. How I longed to slam that door shut and at the same time I wanted to jump up and leave. But that was something I could not do. Instead I clenched my fists so tightly my nails made red crescents on my palms. My hands were shaking and I was unaware that every few seconds I was twisting and snapping the telltale elastic bands on my wrists. However, we only talked about that several weeks later. Aware of my anxiety, instead of asking me an intrusive question, Ms Travis opened a drawer, took out an ashtray and slid it over to me.

'If you want to smoke you can,' she said. 'I always keep this handy in case it's needed.'

16

CHAPTER TWO

The only sound for a few seconds was the click of my lighter, the soft crackle as the cigarette ignited and the deep breaths whenever I inhaled greedily. Almost instantly the nicotine smoothed my jangled nerves and my body finally began to relax.

'I know they are bad for me,' I said ruefully. 'It's just now.'

'I understand,' she said and a reassuring smile came in my direction.

'Cassie, it's not my job to probe, but to find the root of your problem we have to start in the place where it grows: in other words, your childhood. So let's talk about your family a little. What was your mother like?'

The ease of dealing with that question removed some more of my nervousness. Describing my mother's appearance was not a problem, although finding the right words to explain who she was would be more difficult.

'She was short,' I said. 'A bit dumpy, I suppose. She dressed neatly, usually a skirt and jumper, or on a hot day a blouse. Nothing remarkable really about how she looked. At night her hair was wound round big rollers and in the morning it was backcombed into a beehive. Once up, it hardly moved as she lacquered it so strongly to her head. But I never thought of her as my mother really. I mean, I knew she was, but she never acted maternal-like or anything.'

'Can you tell me a little more?'

'She was not a nice woman. Cruel, she was. The only affection I ever saw her show was to my father. Oh, occasionally to my younger brother, but never to me or my older one. No, the only person I think she loved was her husband.'

I hoped as I spoke that I would not be asked questions about him – I was not ready to talk about my father then. I think she understood for no unwanted questions followed. More confidently, I carried on explaining how my mother had been: her black moods, her spite, her laziness. Even walking to the shops was a chore for her. I was hardly at school age when she sent me off with a list of what she wanted. Mainly cigarettes.

I felt a spurt of anger as I talked about her. 'She pandered to my father,' I blurted out. 'Cooked him nice meals served at the table, whereas we children were offered little more than snacks that we ate standing up.

'Her excuse for that was that she had paid for us to have our main meal at school, so we did not need much more. We could smell it though, her cooking, and then we were told to make a sandwich.

'I've never understood why she had children. She never cared for us. If we fell over and scraped our knees she just told us to get up and not make a fuss. Then in the evenings, if it was too dark to go outside, we were sent to our rooms – after we had washed up their dinner plates, that was. Television was for her and my father; she did not want us sitting with them.'

Once I started talking, I managed to say all of that to her, scarcely drawing breath.

She asked about the house I had grown up in, explaining that she was trying to get a clearer picture, not just of my family, but my surroundings as well.

Describing that did not give me a problem either. I told her there was little to say about it. It had four bedrooms, the smallest one being mine, and I described the dark wallpaper downstairs, the sitting room that reeked of stale cigarettes. A brown settee with several burn marks, where my mother, whose interest in housework was negligible, spent most of her time. There was no daytime television then, so she listened to the radio, read her magazines or painted her nails while issuing orders to us children from the moment we were in the house.

There were two prints, in cheap black frames, on the walls: one of a little girl with a dog by her side and the other a blond-haired boy crying. Apart from a couple of chairs the only other furniture was a sideboard where my mother's 'good plates', as she called them, were kept. They only put in an appearance when my grandparents came to visit. It was basically a dreary house, devoid of laughter and care.

Outside was no better; slimy clumps of grass, with pieces of car engines littering the small space outside the back door. There was a shed, which when we were small, we were forbidden to enter. Wanting to turn my thoughts away from that shed, I paused then. For there was a time I had been made to go there and I wanted to push such thoughts straight out of my mind.

If she noticed my voice drying up as I rattled off those details, she made no comment, just swiftly tried to guide my recollections.

'Your brothers, how did you get on with them?' And just that simple question caused a lump to rise in my throat and my eyes welled up.

'All right,' she added quickly, seeing my distress, 'we can talk about them later.'

'It's difficult to remember everything in order,' I told her. 'I might say I was four or five when something happened then later it comes to me that I was older. Everything gets jumbled in my head when I try and go back to those years when I was a child.'

'Why do you think that is, Cassie?'

'I suppose because there was little to mark those early days. My grandmother read to me sometimes, but my mother never did, so I cannot even think of favourite stories.'

'Tell me a little about your grandparents then.'

'They were kind to us children when we visited. Their house smelt different too. All lovely appetising cooking smells and furniture polish. A proper dinner was placed on the table and my grandmother always asked if we wanted seconds.

'"Don't like waste," she would say to us and we dived in all right.

'And when we were finished, it was the grown-ups that cleared the table and washed up. We were told to either go outside to play or sometimes we would watch television. I suppose that was my only glimpse of normality, how it could have been.'

'But in your home there was nothing like that?'

'No. And there were no planned treats either, so I can't close my eyes and see a day at the seaside or something pleasurable we all did as a family, and remember when and where it was.

'We were not made a fuss of on our birthdays either. I was never given a pretty dress to wear and made to feel like a little princess. Except, that is, on my fifth – I remember that well. My grandmother baked a cake for me, brought it over to our house with prettily wrapped presents. A school satchel was one of them. So yes, I remember that birthday.'

What I did not say to her then was that apart from that special day, most of what I can recall about those early years is the constant fear I felt.

Fear of a woman who only shouted at me.

Fear of my eldest brother who pinched me in soft places and pulled my hair.

Fear of not being able to stop the tears, tears that made the woman I called Mum angry.

Then there was the man, the one who sat at the table with a stick by his side. One he raised to hit out at us when we annoyed him.

He was called Dad.

He was, I understood long before I had learnt the vocabulary to express myself, a man who must be obeyed.

'What did your father do for a living, Cassie?'

I had been waiting for her to bring him up, but I was still not ready for it.

'He was a self-employed car mechanic,' was the answer I gave, hoping my tone of voice would tell her to leave it there.

As I spoke an image of my father crept uninvited into my mind, one that was frozen in time. It belonged to my childhood memories, not my adult ones. Every time my subconscious conjures him up, he always appears the same. I see him always as he was before he grew older, when age thinned his brilliantine slicked-back dark hair, placed deep lines bracketing his mouth and beer coarsened his once-slim body. What I remember most though is not so much what he looked like, but that smell of car grease, petrol and cigarettes that not only clung to him but seeped into his very pores, or so it seemed. Those days as a child it was my nose more than his stealthy footsteps that warned me he was near.

Those were the thoughts I did not share, not that day.

'Those,' I told her, 'are my earliest memories. Now, can I ask you a question?'

She nodded encouragingly.

'When do you think the first memory is lodged in a baby's brain? Is it when they leave a dark safe place and come into a world full of noise and light?'

'Why do you ask that question, Cassie?'

'I just wondered if they feel fear then, or is it a learnt emotion?'

'Cassie, all I can tell you is that the early weeks, months and years are important. That is when the seeds for their future are sown.'

'So at what age do those destructive emotions start?' I asked.

'Destructive emotions?'

'Yes, like rage and resentment.'

'When do *you* think they do, Cassie?'

'The moment the adult world betrays them, I guess.'

'Are you thinking of your own childhood now, or the years when you were a mother?' she asks, expecting a reply, but that was another question I did not want to answer.

It was she who told me to write down everything I could remember.

'Start with your early memories,' she said.

'The before?'

'Yes, Cassie – the before.'

Chapter Three

Whenever I try and think about before that is before he made me feel dirty and ashamed, before that terrible secret was mine to carry, my mind goes blank. It is when I'm asleep that those memories visit me, catching the end of a dream, forcing me awake.

I have come to understand that there are two Cassies: the one before and the one after.

The little girl who was denied what other small children grow up expecting is their right – being nursed when ill, cuddled, played peekaboo with and made to believe in Father Christmas and fairies – was still blessed with a happy disposition. In that at least she was lucky, otherwise she might have lost her childhood almost as soon as she was born.

But despite her mother's lack of care, her father's red-hot rages, she clung tenaciously to some of the joy of life that small children possess. Seeing a delicately coloured butterfly, a bright-eyed bird or next-door's fluffy cat, all things that to an adult were commonplace, to that little girl they were brand new and each sighting filled her with excitement. That was the Cassie of 'Before'.

'There are always some happy memories in our past,' my therapist had told me. 'Search for them as well as the bad ones.' She pointed out that there had been people I loved: my grandparents and my baby brother.

'And Cassie, when you come again, you can tell me a little about your older brother as well.'

That week I did as she asked and tried to put my thoughts in order and commit them to paper.

Reflections on my older brother made me uncomfortable, part embarrassment mixed with a dollop of pity and shame that I still felt the power of the first. Even as a small child I knew he was not the same as other children. Skinny-limbed, with knobbly knees and elbows and a mouth moistened by drops of saliva that never seemed to close. Even as a child he was far from attractive. When chastised, which was often, he would just look bewildered. If one of our parents harangued him even more harshly than normal, he would sit, head hanging down to his chest, a long thread of drool dangling from his mouth, his thin arms wrapped around his body for comfort. It seemed that everything he did irritated them. His walk was clumsy, his mouth slack, but it was the expressions in his eyes that caused my distress. Depending on the atmosphere around him they were sometimes hopeful, but far more often they were hurt and terrified. He did not understand what it was he had done to anger an adult into raising their hand to him. Those times I would watch with a combination of fear and pity as his body would shake while piercing, keening cries came out of his mouth.

Maybe he knew all along that all he had done wrong was to be born.

I have tried to block many of my memories of him from my mind. Child or not, I still feel that I should have looked out for him more. And it is guilt that sometimes swamps me, for even when I was older I did little to help him. I never saw who he really was: an unhappy toddler trapped in a growing boy's body.

It was only when I started school that I realised his name was Ben.

Up until then I had thought it was Moron.

The love I had inside me was reserved for my grandparents and my baby brother, Jimmy. From the first moment I saw him, a tiny pink-faced scrap, I felt a wave of protectiveness and love. I loved hearing his soft snuffling as he slept, his tiny face scrunched up, and when he cried, making his round, rosy-cheeked face crumple, I could hardly bear it. It seemed to open up a chasm full of sorrow inside me. I felt that he should be happy all the time and knew that it was the underlying anger in the house that caused those fat tears to fall. Once he could crawl and then totter, my mother had no patience with either his laughter or his cries.

'Cassie, take him outside,' she would scream impatiently. 'He's under my feet. I'm trying to get your father's dinner ready. Can't stand that noise he's making, and he's under my feet all the time.' She did not seem at all bothered that the floor was filthy and slippery with grease or that drawers left carelessly open might catch his fingers or cut his face if he caught the corner of them.

'Come, Jimmy,' I would say, 'let's go into the garden,' and every time I stretched my hand out to him, his warm little fingers would curl around mine.

A dimpled smile that touched my heart would lift the corners of his mouth, as his tears quickly dried. Podgy little legs tottered beside me as opening the back door we went into what passed for a garden. Out there would be a child's tea service, given me by my grandmother, which was kept in the old pram that all three of us had been taken out in at different times.

In front of it I placed my doll, also a present from her.

'All little girls need dolls,' she had said when she handed me a parcel wrapped in colourful paper. Undoing it, I had found 'Jane' as I was to call her, blonde hair with eyes that opened and shut. Tucked beside her was an assortment of paraphernalia my grandmother said was necessary when caring for a doll. My eyes, she recounted, looked like stars that day, so brightly did they shine the moment I first saw that doll. Maybe deep down, in a place she was too frightened to visit, she guessed what I needed was both friends and more parental love and care.

The doll was my constant companion. Every day I brushed her hair, dressed her in her pretty frock, and at night I wiped her face and changed her into a nightdress.

That was who I was before: a little girl who looked forward to visits to her grandmother, playing with her baby brother and finding old copies of her mother's magazines that she would flick through, her fingers tracing the pictures inside the shiny covers. Unfortunately that little girl had a very short life. And the person she might have grown up into never did live.

A year ago I walked to the park. Being a mile or so from where I lived, few of my neighbours visited it. Children of all ages were shrieking with excitement as they bounced on the see-saws, climbed onto swings and played all the games that so long ago, when I was their age, the children in our neighbourhood had also played.

A memory floats into my head so crystal clear every little detail stands out.

A young mother is holding a small child by the hand. She had taken her to the pond where moorhens were teaching their fluffy black chicks self-sufficiency. I watched as she gave the child some bread to throw. No sooner had it landed than the moorhens, wings beating the water furiously, moved towards it. Dipping their heads down, they greedily gobbled up every morsel. The child clapped her hands in glee, her face one big smile. I had thought then that if I had a camera, I could have captured the delight only the very young feel. Then I would have had it blown up to the size of a painting and called it 'Childhood'.

Chapter Four

Having been made to think of my time before I was forced to carry the burden of my secret brings a certain man to mind. Not that his visits to our estate affected my life when I was a child, but it shows how we, who lived there, were.

Ours was a street where people liked to say they minded their own business. Of course that did not mean there was no gossip, for rest assured there was plenty; and the more salacious the better. But there was little concern for others or their circumstances.

If a man lost his job, the bosses were blamed. When school leavers could not find employment, no matter how often they played truant and how few qualifications they had to their name, the government was blamed. And a woman sporting a black eye must, they muttered behind her back, have surely deserved it for wasn't her husband a hard-working man? The tutting and raised eyebrows knew no limit should a young, unmarried girl become pregnant. Without any questions being asked, a label woven out of spite and innuendo bearing the words 'dirty little whore' was pinned on her. Both she and the mother would be blamed. Neither poverty nor marriages to men who spent much of their wages in the pub united the women there. Instead, like a flock of caged hens, chests puffed up with righteous indignation, they pecked away ruthlessly at the reputations of those even more unfortunate than themselves.

It was to that street that the man arrived. He did not seem to be of much importance – he was just a man with a sad little daughter, who brought us eggs. With only the one nearby shop, serving little more than cigarettes and newspapers, the man who delivered fresh eggs was welcome in our road. In addition, those families who had allotments were able to make cash by selling fresh vegetables to him to take to London.

There were other necessities in his cart: packets of tea, sugar, loaves of bread and biscuits. Sometimes even a scraggy chicken whose egg-laying days had come to an end was offered. With him arriving in the week and the fish and chip man every Friday, we had little need to venture into town.

Each week I would hear his horn blast out and my mother, hardly bothering to raise herself from wherever she was sitting, would glance in my direction.

'Pass me my bag, Cassie,' she would say each time, although with just a slight stretch she could have easily managed that task herself. And I, anxious not to displease her, for although slow at housework she was quick to administer stinging slaps, would stop whatever I was doing, scramble to where it lay on the floor, usually inches from her hand, and pass it to her. Placing it on her lap, she would grope inside its depths before pulling out a few coins or a crumpled note.

CHAPTER FOUR

'Now go and fetch the eggs, get the usual dozen,' she said each time and, clutching the money, I would make for the door. As I reached it her voice buzzed in my ears as she repeated the sentence she said every time: 'Don't drop them, mind, Cassie, or no supper for you.'

The man made me feel uncomfortable. If I was first to get to the cart a smile showing discoloured teeth would flash in my direction. 'Hallo, pretty little girlie, now what can I do for you on this lovely day?' he would say when there was no one to hear him and a wink would follow. I disliked the feel of his calloused hands touching mine when I handed over the coins. They seemed to linger too long on my flesh. 'Soft little hands,' he would remark then, as his finger ran slowly across them.

I noticed his daughter and one look told me she was also 'different', just as Ben was. She might have been older than me, but she was not much taller. I never saw a smile on her round face nor did I ever hear her speak. Only high-pitched squeals occasionally came out of her mouth. Instinct told me even then that he was not a man to be kind to someone like her. Each time I saw her I felt her sadness.

I once asked her what her name was. At this the man looked angry. 'She's daft, isn't she?' he said. 'She can't talk. Useless, she is. But I look after her all right. Isn't that right?' he said to her, giving her knee a firm squeeze. I saw her cringe and understood she did not like his touch either. Then I had no understanding of what the real reason for her despair might have been.

I did not believe him when he said he looked after her well. 'Shut up with your noise,' I heard him say more than once to her. I don't think he gave her any care. Even my brother Ben sometimes forgot our mother's resentment of him and smiled and there were also occasions when he burst out laughing at some of our little brother Jimmy's antics. Not that child. I did not believe then, and I certainly don't now, that any laughter had ever come out of her mouth. With her unbrushed hair and tatty clothes, she appeared completely neglected.

'She's not right in the head,' said the neighbours as if this justified the neglect.

'Like bloody Ben, she is,' said my mother. 'Can't get away from idiots, can I?' The daughter's presence gave her yet another excuse not to go out to the cart. 'Can't bear looking at another one – you go, Cassie,' she was prone to say, especially it seemed when Ben was in the room and a satisfied smirk would cross her face when she saw he had understood her.

Then one day the man failed to turn up. I listened for the sound of his bell, but there was only silence.

'Blast that man! I was going to have ham and eggs tonight. Already told your father. Now what are we going to have?' my mother muttered crossly, not expecting an answer. 'Ah, get off that lazy arse of yours, Cassie! You can walk down to the shop. They'll have eggs, just not fresh ones. Just make sure they don't try and palm you off with cracked ones, mind.'

I scurried down the road, the coins held tightly in my hand, down to the row of shops. She was right: they had eggs, just not the large brown ones the egg man had. Instead they were the small white ones with thin shells.

Walking back carefully, knowing if I tripped and one egg was broken I would feel my mother's hand stinging across the backs of my legs, I wondered why the man with his sad little daughter had not come that day. Did she have a mother at home? If so, what was she like, sending the child out every day with her father? I had never heard anyone ask that question nor express any concern as to her well-being. No one would have thought of asking if the child's mother was around.

It was not until nearly a week later that we learnt the shocking truth of why the man's cart had not arrived. He had been arrested and was held in police custody: the charge was murder. The victim's face was splashed across the newspapers. A 15-year-old schoolgirl had been sexually assaulted and strangled.

'Not that simpleton that was always with him then,' was my father's only comment.

The neighbours, though, had much more to say. Standing on the street in groups, leaning over back fences, they were simply agog with the news. 'We could all have been murdered in our beds,' said one. 'Our children taken,' added another.

'To think those coins he gave us had been touched by his grimy, evil, murdering hands,' said my mother.

Women shuddered; voices were shrill.

I heard them saying no doubt our street would be crawling with journalists.

'They might want to interview us and then it will be our photographs in the papers,' said the women with an undercurrent of avaricious glee in their voices. And for the next few days not one woman was to be seen with her hair scrunched up in rollers and battered carpet slippers on her feet. But the journalists had no more interest in our community than the women had about the welfare of the sad little girl who sat beside the man selling eggs.

I often wonder what happened to her. I can only hope that someone cared for her more lovingly than he had.

Chapter Five

How do I describe the life on the estate I grew up in? After all, it was much the same as so many others that had been hastily built in city areas when the slums had been demolished. Yes, the houses had more space and the lavatory was inside, but what the town planners had not taken into account was how communities looked after each other. Families had become divided, no mother lived just around the corner, free to babysit at a moment's notice. Old family friends no longer lived next door, nor was there a corner shop run by a couple who, knowing everyone in the street, gave credit for food and sold cigarettes separately when times were hard. A notebook under the counter kept the accounts. No need for references, trust was what counted.

I am sure when the families I grew up knowing first moved in, they had only seen the pluses. But by the time I was old enough to notice, a pall of defeat hung over our estate. Little about our surroundings was uplifting, just row after row of red-bricked houses with the same coloured doors, built on streets lacking in any form of greenery. When the occupants were first given keys, they had expected that within a few months there would be a large supermarket, a comfortable family pub, a community hall and a park with a generous play area for the children, all of which would practically be on their doorstep. All of which failed to materialise. The only useful amenities were four shops. One selling out-of-date goods, tinned food, cigarettes, fizzy drinks, sweets and newspapers; a post office where dole cheques could be cashed; a charity shop stuffed with old clothes, dog-eared paperbacks and scratched vinyl records; and a launderette with four coin-operated machines.

There was an old dilapidated pub that remained standing on a street corner while the houses around it were turned into mounds of rubble. For some reason it escaped the bulldozers. Rumour has it that cash had changed hands. It was certainly frequented by some very unsavoury-looking men. It was a dark smoky place, where women did not feel welcome, not somewhere they could dress up and go to on a Saturday night and sit with their friends while their husbands played darts or talked amongst themselves about sport.

There was no youth club for the teenagers and, without a community hall, the social groups the children and teens could have joined, such as the Scouts and the Girl Guides, had nowhere to meet. So the streets became our playground until the harsh winter set in.

As the days shortened, iron-grey clouds hung in the sky and bored children huddled discontentedly inside their homes. Televisions threw flickering blue light onto thin curtains, cars were left unwashed and scraggy cats slunk around the over-spilling dustbins. Waking to frozen dawns, icy air nipping our noses and toes, we would dress hurriedly before going down the stairs to hastily swallow some breakfast before making our way to school.

Once March blew itself out, it was time to turn the streets back into our playground again. Skipping ropes were brought outside and chalk or crayons used to draw squares on pavements ready for Hopscotch to commence. Sullen youths, hair slicked back, hands deep in the pockets of their imitation leather jackets, filter-less Woodbines dangling from thin lips, slouched in corners, stared blankly at the teenage girls meandering past.

In the school holidays, once the men had left for work, breakfast had scarcely been swallowed before my contemporaries shot out of their homes in search of their playmates. Although the Moors murders had taken place some years earlier, between 1963 and 1965, the memory of them still lingered. We had become the generation that had to be watched. Mothers instructed their children never to get into an unknown car, not to take sweets from a stranger – in fact, not to talk to anyone at all. 'Not even a woman they added,' thinking of Myra Hindley. After those instructions they let their offspring out onto the streets. Once I had finished whatever chores my mother had for me, I would join them.

Those warm days encouraged the women to leave their doors open, bring cups of tea out to drink on their steps, while they gossiped with those from the houses on either side. There they could watch the smaller children play, content in the belief that this kept them safe. They could see them and any stranger would be spotted, wouldn't he?

But there was one amongst them who knew it was not the stranger who was the danger. She knew who the real monster was. He was the man who shared her bed, sat at her table, the one who had fathered her children. The one waiting for his daughter to grow just a little bit more.

She answered to several names. Her husband called her 'Lizzy', her parents 'Elizabeth'. I had another name for her: it was 'Mum'.

Chapter Six

My therapist wanted to delve into my early memories so I made notes about my school days. For that was where my feelings of isolation really began.

When I started school, it was not so much what happened on my first day there, it's what didn't that is imprinted on my mind. That morning, surrounded by a pack of small, neatly dressed children, holding onto their parents' hands, our teacher came out to greet the new arrivals. Wearing a dark blue denim skirt and a cream shirt, her light brown hair tied back, wire-rimmed glasses perched on a small nose, a warm smile on unmade-up lips, she stood in front of our group and introduced herself as Miss Davis. Looking back, I can see now that she was a pretty young woman, fresh out of teacher training college. In fact, I later learnt that our school had been her first teaching post. But to a class of five-year-olds who thought anyone out of their early teens was no longer young, we did not see either her newness or her prettiness, she was 'Miss', a person we understood instinctively had to be respected. I watched as she walked up to each small group, chattered to the mothers, leaning down to talk to the children, then lastly walked over to where my mother and I were standing a little apart from the rest. Even then I sensed reluctance in her steps, a sudden falseness to her smile.

'Mrs Cook,' she said brightly, 'and you,' she added, smiling down at me, 'must be Cassie.' I felt my mother stiffen slightly and was somehow aware that she felt uncomfortable in that schoolyard where few other mothers had even greeted her and none had stood near us. Her hands were firmly tucked into her pockets and there they remained – touching another woman's hand by extending one of hers for a brief handshake was not something she had any intention of doing. Nor did she show any interest in Miss Davis's reassurances that I would enjoy my first day. Those sentiments fell on stony ground. The indifferent expression on my mother's unsmiling face remained firmly in place.

'Well, that's your job, isn't it?' she said gracelessly when Miss Davis's 'welcome to my class' speech came to an end, before shoving me lightly in the back.

'Go with the teacher now, Cassie.'

'I will see you later when you come and collect her,' said Miss Davis, still trying to keep up the pretence of friendliness.

'Not me, you won't. I've got dinner to prepare. She can come home with her brother, Ben. No doubt you know him?' And the smile on my mother's face then was part challenging, part mocking.

I saw by the expression on Miss Davis's face that she knew exactly who my brother was.

'I was not here when he was in the Infants,' she replied, 'so I don't really know him. But Mrs Cook, now he is in the Juniors, it might be a problem for Cassie to walk back with him.'

'Why's that then?'

'The Juniors finish later than the Infants.'

A derisive sound left my mother's mouth, more of a snort than a laugh. 'Well then she can either wait for him or he can be let out early. It's not as though he learns anything, is it?' And with those words she turned on her heel and left me there.

No pat on the head, no little hug or whispered farewells that all around me I could see the other children receiving. Instead all I was left with was the sight of my mother's retreating back. Embarrassed by her behaviour, with burning cheeks I stared down at the ground beneath my feet.

Miss Davis made no comment but just said, 'Time to go into the classroom, Cassie,' and calling out to all the other little children to follow her, I walked beside her as she led the way into the school building.

Trying to remember those early days is difficult. It was, after all, a long time ago and so much has happened since. A shelf by the door had a large number of picture and storybooks out of a child's reach and I took in paints and paintbrushes, things I had only seen before in shop windows.

There were games, a huge box crammed with real toys as opposed to pieces of wood and the smooth stones for skimming in a pond that I was used to, as well as a selection of colouring-in books and wax crayons. It was this last item that caught my interest and seeing me picking them up, Miss Davis asked me if I wanted to colour in the pictures inside the book or draw something myself.

'Draw something,' I answered, not that I had any idea of how to do that.

'All right then, let's see what you can do,' she said encouragingly as she placed a thick piece of paper on my minuscule desk. 'Now, what did you have in mind, Cassie?'

A blank look from me conveyed the message that it was not something I had thought through.

'Well, Cassie, when I was your age the first thing I always drew was a house.' And picking up one of the crayons she placed it in my hand then wrapped hers around it and moved our hands slowly across the paper. And in no time at all a square house complete with windows and a door appeared.

'See, that wasn't too difficult now, was it? Now try and do it on your own.'

At first my fingers, which had never held a pencil before, were clumsy, but by the end of the day, with a little more help I had managed to draw an almost square house with a chimney in the middle of the roof, a patch of green at the side, a row of yellow circles depicting flowers and a brown blur that vaguely resembled a leafless tree.

I must have conjured up those last images from seeing the gardens of the new houses being laid and planted.

'Very good, Cassie,' Miss Davis said with a smile and I, bathing in that unaccustomed praise, felt my face warm with pleasure.

At five years old I had completed my first drawing. I was proud of it. At last I might have done something to win my mother's approval. My teacher rolled it up neatly and placed it in my satchel.

'Now, give that to your mother when you get home. I'm sure she will want to see it.'

When the bell rang, and the teacher told us that school was over for the day, there were squeals of excitement as the class emptied. Small children, bursting to tell their mothers all about their first day, pulled on their blazers, picked up their satchels and rushed excitedly to the door.

'Walk, don't run,' Miss Davis reminded them as she escorted them outside.

In the playground were the mothers, their mouths stretched into wide smiles. And as though their offspring had disappeared into a swirling vortex and were only now being returned to them they knelt, all ready for their children to hurtle into their outstretched arms. I watched the hugs and embraces given, heard the chatter of small children before I walked over to where Ben was waiting for me (Miss Davis must have arranged for his teacher to let him out of Juniors early).

He, looking more awkward than ever, was standing as far away from everyone as he could possibly be. I noticed the odd glance from the mothers going in his direction. Did they see his difference as a threat? Not that this was a thought that came into my mind when I was five, but when I was older it did. I was just wishing it were anyone but him who was waiting for me.

'Let's go, Cassie,' he said with his goofy smile and slow speech and I, feeling guilty at my disloyal thoughts, slipped my hand in his. He was my big brother and it was not his fault that he was different. I think at that moment he was proud to act the part of my protector. Then he was a gentle boy – the changes in him came later.

My mother was not, as she had told the teacher, cooking dinner when we returned home. As usual she was sitting on the settee, a cigarette in her hand, a mug of tea by her side and a magazine on her lap. If I was expecting her to ask how my first day was and what I had done I was disappointed: she showed no interest. Hardly raising her eyes as she said, 'Oh, you're back then,' she continued flipping through her magazine. But my baby brother thoroughly made up for her disinterest. His eyes widened in pleasure as soon as I walked in. I hugged his plump little body and was rewarded by a beaming smile.

'Maybe this time I've done something to please my mother as well,' I thought hopefully as, reaching into my satchel, I brought out my drawing.

'Look, Mum,' I said, 'I did this for you at school,' and handed her the rolled-up picture. 'Teacher said it was good,' I told her, standing impatiently on one foot, waiting to hear that she finally liked something I had done.

'Pleased she thinks so,' my mother said. 'What does she think I would want to do with it? I have enough mess with all your father's stuff coming into the house as it is.' Then hardly giving it another glance, she condemned it to a piece of rubbish by picking it up with one finger and thumb before marching into the kitchen and throwing it in the already overflowing bin.

Any faint hope I might have had that it would have been hung proudly on the wall disappeared. If I had thought that the picture would suddenly turn her into a mother who would sit me down and ask questions about my first day at school, I was to be disappointed. Nothing was said about what I had done there, not one question asked. I was just told to change out of my school clothes and help her in the kitchen. 'You can wash up those teacups when you come down,' she told me, which I was only just about capable of. Even though I was tall for my age, I had to stand on tiptoe to reach into the basin.

Supper that evening was beans on toast for my brothers and me and ham, eggs and chips for my parents. My stomach growled when I watched them wipe their plates clean with fried bread and smack their lips as the last morsel was finished. There was still a congealed pile of those little orange beans that I had come to loathe left on my plate and picking up my fork, I forced some into my mouth.

Ours was not a household where pushing unwanted food to one side would have been tolerated. If my father was in a good mood we would just be told about how children in other countries went to bed hungry; if in a bad one, then just a grimace of distaste would cause his hand to grip his stick. If within seconds the food did not reach our mouths, the stick would be swished down on whichever part of the child in question was nearest him.

It was those actions, of my parents and the atmosphere in the house, that dimmed the brightness of any good memories I might have tucked away. Ones that in later life I could have looked back on with nostalgia.

I think I quite enjoyed my first year at school. After all, there was little in the way of conventional lessons. Instead of having to learn words and the times tables by reciting them over and over until they were lodged in our memories, Miss Davis disguised them as games.

Our teacher had a book, *Teach Your Baby to Read*. We all giggled when she told us the title. 'Babies can't read,' we said. She did not contradict us but instead went ahead with the method used inside it: large cards, one side showing a picture and the other side the word. We were shown first the pictures then the words. After that the cards were shuffled and we had to see how many words we were able to recognise without the picture. Giving a wrong answer was never criticised so we were encouraged to raise our hands and try.

It did not take long for us to begin to recognise the letters. By the time we had been in her class for a few weeks whole words became familiar and we felt we were really reading. That, we were told, was a big achievement.

Adding up and subtracting was something else that, using the same method, she succeeded in teaching us. Then when I went to the shops I was able to check if the change was correct – that must have been the only thing I learnt at school that my mother thought useful.

It was when I moved up to the Juniors that everything started to change. Our new teacher, Miss Roberts, dressed in a dark suit, hair in a tight French pleat, horn-rimmed glasses perched on a rather long nose and a pursed mouth that seemed to open only to heap scorn on small shoulders, had little patience for Miss Davis's modern methods. She made it clear that she did not think of lessons as fun: we were in school to learn, not play, was the message drummed into us daily.

Reading changed from learning with pictures into long tedious hours where lists of words for us to learn were handed out daily. We were expected to be able to spell each and every one by the following morning. Our day started out with a test and mistakes were severely criticised. Arithmetic lessons were even worse, the class sat straight-backed, arms on desks as like so many parrots we recited the times tables over and over in our droning child voices.

As well as dismissing the idea that learning could be enjoyable, Miss Roberts relished in catching us out making, as she called them, 'sloppy mistakes'. Smudged or crooked writing was held up for the whole class to see and when a question was shot out and the person picked on to answer gave the wrong one, an exasperated sigh would precede a strong rebuke. No longer did my arm shoot up. Mistakes were not acceptable, Miss Roberts told us more than once, and I did not want to be the child who publicly made one.

We were also meant to be a credit to the school. Always walk sedately, be neat and clean, and hair must be combed back neatly into place before being secured by a ribbon or a slide.

It did not take long for our Miss Roberts to look at me with the same disdain I had seen more than once on teachers' faces when my brother's name was mentioned.

'Why can't you comb your hair neatly, Cassie? Tell your mother it needs washing and your skirt needs ironing. Have you not noticed your shirt has a stain on it? Change it for a clean one. Tomorrow I want to see an improvement.'

The list of what was wrong with my appearance seemed endless. Even worse, the teacher did not say all of that in private. She always seemed to wait until there were more than one pair of ears listening, which made those remarks fodder for my classmates' taunts, which they had no problem using.

The improvements the teacher asked for did not, as I had expected, send my mother into an incoherent rage. Instead they were greeted with supercilious mockery.

'Hair gets washed on Friday, you know that, Cassie. Your skirt needs ironing? Well, do it yourself. Oh I forgot you're not big enough to reach yet. Well, I'm not your maid.'

'And the shirt?'

'You get a clean one on Mondays, don't you?'

I did not have the courage to point out that having just one shirt meant I only had it clean if the washing had been done over the weekend. And that was not always the case. Words I knew better than to utter. So I stood silently while she had her say.

'Think your dad and I are made of money, that you can have a shirt for every day? You're little Miss Muck now, are you? Mixing too much with those children from the new houses, aren't you? Getting fancy ideas from them, I'm sure!'

The truth was I was not mixing with anyone. There were children from our estate at the school who, if I was not seen walking home with Ben, might have been friendlier. But no sooner did they notice him than they gave me a wide berth. This was an admission I was not going to give my mother the satisfaction of hearing.

Ordinary lessons were hard enough but whatever embarrassment I was made to feel about my appearance was multiplied ten times over when I entered the gym. Changing in front of the other girls was an ordeal I dreaded. My knickers, instead of being the uniform blue of the school, were more grey than white and my vest worn thin in places was a good match for them. The gym teacher made no comment, she didn't have to, and the expression on her face said it all. I had seen her glance at me before looking away.

She was one of those who did not see a neglected child from a poor home. Just a grubby one she felt an aversion for.

Chapter Seven

It was not until I had met my therapist for the third time that the subject we both knew I was there to discuss was finally raised: my childhood secret had to be talked about. The second secret I had, the adult one, I was determined never to reveal.

I had though been fully aware, ever since I had been handed the card with the time of my appointment on it, that she wanted me to bring it up and was waiting until I felt I was ready. And I? I was waiting for the question – when did I become aware that the affection my father gave me was unnatural? For if I had been told and I had, never to talk about it, there had to be a reason. And I must have worked out the answer at a fairly young age. However, she asked me instead how old I was when he first touched me in an inappropriate way.

'Somewhere between six and seven,' I answered without hesitation.

She waited for me to elaborate and knowing I could not put her off any longer, filled in some of the blanks in the notes she had on me. Since my first appointment I had forced those painful memories out into my consciousness and then stored them in my mind, ready to tell her. And that was the day. Oh, I had already in my life admitted to being abused three times, but never before had I shared the facts of how and when.

At five I was not completely ignorant about the differences between girls and boys. I had seen both my brothers naked, so was aware of what lay between their legs. It raised curiosity more than repugnance when I was a child. That little thing I had seen bobbing in the bath reminded me of wrinkled cockles: neither pretty nor ugly, just something I did not have. I understood it was only to be taken out when boys need to pee. But then apart from when I was getting ready for bed, my knickers stayed in place as well. So I seldom gave our differences much thought, apart from being envious on more than one occasion, when my need to relieve myself sent me running to the nearest bush for cover.

Under its dubious, quite often prickly shelter, I had to endure the palaver of downing knickers, from under my skirt, at the same time as taking care not to expose too much of my body. Each time I squatted down, I tingled with fear of someone suddenly appearing. It certainly made me empty my bladder as fast as possible on those occasional journeys into the countryside. No, peeing outside was not relaxing for girls, I decided. But for boys, well, that was an entirely different story. No sooner were they jigging about, hands on the part of their trousers where that little thing lay, they made it unashamedly clear what their need was. All they were told was to turn their backs and relieve themselves against a tree, hedge or bush. Then out came their little spouts and within seconds a pale golden arc splattered the grass. Once they had rid themselves of every drop with a nonchalant shrug, it was tucked back into their trousers.

What I had not given any thought to was what happened when we grew bigger. I had no idea that that small wrinkled little thing would grow as the body did. Nor what other uses than peeing it was put to. But those days of not knowing were swiftly drawing to an end. And once they did, that part of my brothers that made us different would cease to look innocent.

The first time my father showed me a different sort of affection it was over so quickly that although it left me feeling uneasy, I was not frightened – not then. I had literally bumped into him on the landing at the top of the stairs. I was coming from my bedroom, where I was fetching my doll, and he from the bathroom. His hand was still zipping up his trousers when the other one caught hold of me.

'What's the rush, Cassie?' he said, pulling me in so close I could hardly breathe. But that did not stop me inhaling that particular aroma that always clung to him. The usual combination of stale cigarette smoke, oil and car grease that day had the additional overtones of sour beer. 'You're turning into a pretty little girl,' he said while one hand still held me close in what I thought at that moment was a fatherly hug. The fingers of his other hand stroked my cheek and enjoying his rare show of affection, I turned my face into his hand and nestled it there. His fingers continued to stroke me and he whispered again that I was turning into a pretty little girl. I am sure then that if I could have turned myself into a small creature, a kitten perhaps, I would have purred with contentment.

Then something changed, his breath quickened and I felt my body being lifted, my bottom supported by his knee. Instead of the warm caress I had been enjoying, firm fingers circled my chin, tilted my face up and bending down, he fastened his lips over mine. His hot, damp mouth with a tongue that worked on parting my lips, before the tip of it slid into my mouth. I wriggled, tried to push my small fists against his chest; I did not like what was happening, I wanted him to stop.

'Shush,' was all he said, his breath tickling my ear, 'shush now.' Now that hand instead of stroking my cheek covered my mouth, stifling any sounds I might have made. Pushing his knee under my bottom he raised me higher until I was several inches off the floor. I could hardly move; with my back against the wall and his knee forcing my legs apart, I was powerless. It was over in just a matter of seconds. He straightened up, stood away from me and without his support I slid down the wall onto the floor.

'Come, Cassie, up you get,' and his hand grasped mine and pulled me to my feet.

My legs almost buckled with the sudden fear that was coursing through my body. By his action he had shown me a part of the adult world that I was far too young to see. I wanted to creep into my bedroom, pull the covers over my head and pretend it had never happened.

'I think you like your dad, don't you, Cassie? Tell me you do.'

My nostrils were again filled with the smell of his breath, hot and rancid. And there was a new smell, that of his excitement and my fear.

'Yes,' I whispered, for what else could a young child say? He was my father, I did not want him to get angry with me. I recognised that his voice was mocking me and glancing up from under my lashes I saw a small sly smile on his face that somehow scared me more than the frightening scowls I had seen all too often.

Tears started to fill my eyes as I looked up at him speechlessly. What had seemed so nice earlier now made me tremble. My doll was lying near my side. I had dropped her and all I wanted to do then was pick her up, make sure she was not hurt and get away from him as fast as possible.

Noticing my movement, he put his arm round my shoulder and gave it a gentle squeeze.

'Now, don't start making a fuss, Cassie. Nothing to it, just means you are special to me. Now, don't be telling your friends, they might be jealous. We'll keep this as our secret, right? Right, Cassie?'

'Yes, Dad.'

'Now, there's my good girl.' Again he lifted my chin until his dark eyes met mine and I, like a baby rabbit caught in the yellow gleam of oncoming headlights, stood motionless.

'Means I like you more than your brothers, don't forget that,' and a gentle kiss was dropped onto the top of my head. 'Now, come on downstairs' Another small hug, and he was gone.

I picked up my doll, straightened her clothes, then my own and silently went downstairs.

If my mother had heard or even sensed that something had happened, she gave no indication.

'You can put that doll down and make yourself useful. Put the kettle on and get the mugs and milk out. You've not forgotten how to pour hot water over teabags, have you?'

'No.'

'Good, I need to put my feet up,' and a malicious smile came in my direction.

Hatred bubbled inside me. 'Lazy, ugly cow' were the words in my head.

'Yes, Mum,' were the ones that came out of my mouth.

Chapter Eight

I was very wary of my father after that. Prickles of unease crawled over my body whenever I saw him looking at me. I was too young to rationalise what had happened, I just knew I did not want it to happen again.

For a short while he did not come near me. He went several weeks without even losing his temper, which made the atmosphere in the house unusually peaceful. Gradually, as the days passed, I began to relax around him. But that did not last for long.

What happened after that seems blurred. My memories are a kaleidoscope of bright and dim flashes of recall. I remember how he started tiptoeing into my room early in the morning while I was still full of sleep. I recognised the smell of him: it was on the hand that covered my mouth, and in the breath that fell onto my face when he whispered in my ear and even worse, it oozed from his body when he slid under the covers.

'Just a quick cuddle with my special girl,' he said and at the very beginning that's all it was.

That was until my mother decided to take up bingo, going once a week with her friend.

'Off you go to bed, Cassie,' my father would say but not before as a special treat he had allowed me to watch some television and he'd even make me a cup of sweet milky cocoa.

Sitting up in bed, my doll on my lap, I was combing her hair when I heard the creak of the stairs. 'Just him going to the bathroom,' I thought hopefully, a hope that died as he entered my room. He sat on the edge of my bed and ran his fingers through my hair.

'Why aren't you asleep?' he asked and not really knowing, I shrugged.

'I don't know,' I whispered, for he was whispering too.

'Well, if I came in beside you I think that would help, wouldn't it?'

I did not answer. My child's instinct was telling me that I did not want him to. Whereas I might enjoy a cuddle while he sat on my bed, I did not like it when he slid under the covers. But my younger self did not recognise a rhetorical question when she heard one. He was not waiting for my permission, he was just telling me of his intention as, without waiting for my reply, he pulled up the covers and slid under them.

'There,' he said, as he lay behind me, pulling me close into his body. 'That's nice, isn't it?' His hand gently stroked my hair and he told me again that I was special. I could hear his breathing growing deeper, feel his hand running down my body until it reached the hem of my nightdress. It moved under it, until it lay on my stomach. His hands were large, with fine dark hairs on the back, and thinking of what they looked like placed another picture in my mind. I saw a huge spider so big it nearly covered my stomach and was crawling over my bare flesh.

The smell of him was filling my nostrils. I thought if I stayed very still he would believe I was asleep and go. But he didn't. Instead that hand slipped further down until it was in between my legs.

'Still,' I told myself, 'stay still, Cassie, and he will leave.'

I heard his breath quicken, his arm tighten against me. I felt something hard press against my back and still I remained motionless, my eyes squeezed tightly shut.

'There's a good girl,' he said and then he rolled out of my bed.

He tucked my blankets over my shoulders, leant down and kissed the top of my head and then he was gone.

For several days I tried to pretend nothing had happened, that it was just part of a dream. And then he returned, and I knew it was real.

It took him several times of coming to my room where I lay open-eyed and silent before his hands did more than just stroke. This time a finger entered me and it hurt. I clenched my fists and stayed very still, believing that if I did not speak or move then it couldn't be happening, could it? But I knew it was.

'Be a good girl, Cassie, now,' he would say when I winced at the feel of his hands touching my bare skin and running up my legs and under my nightdress.

I wanted to cry out, to tell him not to, but then who would have stopped him? Who would have defended me?

Instinct told me it would not be my mother. So I choked back my protests when his hands disappeared under the cocoon of my bedclothes.

'Don't make me cross,' he whispered the first time when I tried to wriggle away. 'I know you like it.'

But he was wrong, I didn't.

My nightmares began, they visited me nightly, all of them different, but all with the same message: I was helpless. There was one where I was in a dark room. I knew there was a door that opened to a place full of sunlight. I stumbled round the room touching the walls, but however hard I tried, I never found it. In another I was falling, falling through space, my arms flapped in my sleep, my mouth opened to cry out and I woke to my own screams of terror ringing in my ears.

At school, my lessons suffered. I would drift off into my own world instead of listening to the teacher. It was the beginning of those years when fear held me in its grip.

At weekends, my father used another ploy. The first Saturday when he had not come to my room made me almost light-headed with relief. A feeling that was short-lived the moment I went into the kitchen for my breakfast and found him there.

'Oh, Cassie,' he said, 'I'm going to work in the shed. Be a good girl and bring me out a cup of tea, won't you?'

Without meeting my eyes, my mother put the kettle on and I could feel the seconds slipping away as I waited for it to boil. Its whistle told me that my freedom had come to an end.

I watched as she spooned two teaspoons of sugar into a mug before pouring steaming water over the bag. As she carefully stirred the dark liquid before adding a splash of milk, I could feel my heart banging against my ribs.

'Off you go, Cassie. Don't want it getting cold, do we?' and again I would see that tight malicious smile that told me there was no point in protesting.

I found that being in the shed with him was even worse than when he came into my room. There, in that airless space, the stench of tobacco mixed with the smell of oil and grease was so strong, it almost made me retch.

'Your tea, Dad,' I said, standing just inside the door, poised to take flight the moment he took it. He stretched out his arm and instead of taking the mug he caught hold of my dress, laughing at my reluctance to step further into his workroom.

'Not so fast, young lady! Anyone would think you did not want to spend time with your dad. Now, that's not true, is it?'

'No, Dad,' I said obediently before mumbling something about being meant to help my mother. 'Oh, she can wait for a few minutes. You want to make your dad happy, don't you?' And on that Saturday, and most of the ones that followed, I was trapped against the shed's wall while he prodded at the flesh under my skirt as waves of revulsion would rise up from the bottom of my stomach, threatening to choke me.

'When you are a little bit older we can do more nice things that you will like,' he told me each time.

I did not think he had anything in mind that was going to be enjoyable.

*

I waited for my therapist to say something after I had managed to tell her that much.

'I think that is all I can manage today,' I told her, when she remained silent.

'I agree. I knew this would not be easy for you. But Cassie, you telling me is a big breakthrough.'

She offered me some coffee, which she poured from a machine in her office while with trembling hands I lit up another cigarette.

'Tell me how you are feeling now.'

'Guilty,' I said without hesitation, and then I sought the right words to expand on that. 'I feel so guilty. You see, there were times when he was the father I wanted. I know I should have hated him, been totally disgusted by him. But it wasn't always like that. Sometimes he would just put his arm round my shoulders, lightly, not like the other way. Brush my cheek with his hand and tell me I was special. And that made me feel almost happy. And when my mother told me to go to the shops, he would slip me some money to buy sweets. So I felt singled out, that he really meant it when he said I was special to him.

'Was that wrong? I mean ...'

'Cassie, what you have to understand is you were a child, and children are programmed to love their parents, however bad they are. They are still the people whom you were completely reliant on when small. That is when the bond is made that ties a child to its parents. Mostly it is a bond of steel, one that is very hard to break. Many children I have talked to pretend they have two fathers, the nice one and the bad one. That is their way of dealing with it.

'When a child's abuser is the parent, children's feelings are often split. Your father probably did care for you, and he may well have told himself he was doing nothing wrong.'

I said nothing in response to her final words for they had failed to comfort me.

Memories that my therapist wanted me to dig out, look at again and then share with her, I found did not always come chronologically. Their strength, which determines just how clear they are, is not so much influenced by time as by the effect they have had. There had been days – too many of them, I assure you – where those memories were all I had for company. Then I spent hours searching desperately for some glimmer of understanding that would throw light on my father's actions. For maybe if I could understand his, then maybe I could make sense of mine.

As a child he was not the one I hated, but my mother. If his affection was wrong, and I think that I always knew it was, hers was non-existent. Did she ever stroke my hair, cuddle me or even meet my eyes and smile, that mother's smile that speaks without sound of bonding, of friendship and most of all, love? If she did, I have no memory of it.

He, on the other hand, was mercurial in his moods. Yes, there were times when his temper got the better of him and he lashed out, not just at me but my brothers as well. But I also have other memories of those occasions when his good humour was restored and a bag of sweets was handed to me as a present.

'Share them with your brothers and don't eat them all at once,' he would say with a wink, as his hand caressed my head. When business had gone well for him, and a car he had restored had fetched a good price, he would return home in uncustomary high spirits. The moment he walked through the door, his voice shouting out 'hello', told us his day had gone well, as did the smell of fish and chips emanating from the wrapped parcel of newspaper that had our mouths watering with anticipation of this rare treat.

'There's enough for everyone, save you cooking,' he would tell my mother, not that cooking was something she spent much time on. 'Thought we could all watch television together tonight,' he would add, knowing that watching anything, whether a quiz show or a film on that screen, which was so often forbidden by my mother, was another treat we children rarely experienced. It was those little acts of kindness, however rare, that earned him my gratitude. As did seeing the sour expression cross my mother's face, at us being allowed to join them for the evening.

We were so used to her telling us to go to our rooms, that she had put up with us being under her feet for long enough, that we never questioned if that was how other families behaved. What we did know though was that television was something we all wanted to watch. We also knew that once our father had stated we could join them, she would not disagree with him. Pleasing him was even more important than making us miserable, it seemed.

Before I reached my teens and wanted to avoid not just my parents but my brothers as well, I cherished those evenings when, like a normal family, all of us were together. Sitting on the floor, I felt secure enough in my father's good mood to lean against his legs while we watched my mother's favourite programmes, *Coronation Street* being the main one.

Getting away from the house and going for a drive was something else that rarely failed to excite my baby brother and me. My mother though made it clear that, apart from taking her to the shops or to visit her parents, she had no interest in anything to do with cars. In fact the only disagreements between my parents that I remember overhearing were when she complained about the parts of car he brought into the kitchen to work on. The shed was for that, she said, although she still did not see why he had to work from home.

The car factories were expanding and there was plenty of work going there. And not only did they pay well, but their workers received both holiday and sick pay, she pointed out each time she had scoured the local newspaper's situations vacant column. My mother, who might have had little interest in the news, considered herself an expert on the job market, something that easily provoked my father to really lose his temper with her.

'I like being my own boss, not having some jumped-up prat telling me what to do,' was one of his less heated replies.

'People want new cars now,' she pointed out more than once. 'Not those old jalopies that you do up and sell.'

'Oh, why don't you read all of the newspaper then, you stupid woman? Then you might just see that there's been another strike at that factory. Keep that up and all these car businesses will get fed up and start going abroad. There'll be plenty laid off then. There's loads of people wanting to keep their old cars running, which means I'm the one they come to, to get their cars through the MOT. And that gets stricter every year. No, I'm better off doing what I'm doing.'

It was my father's continuation with both 'fixing', as he called it, old cars for their MOTs and buying others that he could make 'as good as new' that resulted in my little brother Jimmy and I going out on drives.

'I'll take the children,' he would say to my mother, though what he meant was that he would only take Jimmy and me. It was as though my father only had two children, for apart from cussing him, I never saw one bit of kindness shown to Ben.

'Oh, ignore the moron,' my father snapped when I, noticing the air of despondency that engulfed Ben on seeing us leave him behind, had tentatively asked if he could come as well. 'I don't want the people I do business with to see him with us. Embarrassing, he is. You'll learn that soon enough. I mean none of the other kids in the street want to play with him, do they? And trust me, you won't want to be seen out with him once you are older. Bad impression he gives. People will think there's something wrong with us. You've already learnt that anyway, haven't you? You know he's the reason nobody wants to walk home from school, don't you?'

I had no answer for him, for I knew it was the truth. But that did not stop me feeling sorry for Ben. Gradually I just accepted that he was not a child who was welcome in other people's homes. Not even his parents'.

I must have been about seven, maybe even a few months younger, when Jimmy and I went on the last drive where I climbed into the car with innocent excitement; that journey is not something I was ever able to eradicate from my memory.

Chapter Nine

It was – not that I realised it then – the real beginning of 'It'. Today we would call it grooming. So I need to force this memory out. Because examining it helps me understand how it was that he was able to exercise so much power over my life.

It was a trip to the country for Jimmy and me, to a small village where a man who sold cars from the patch of land outside his house, lived. My father was delivering one, an old blue Cortina that had been little more than a wreck several weeks earlier. With all the dents knocked out and a new paint job, it looked just as he had said, 'as good as new'.

'Going to deliver that one and pick up another,' he had told my mother.

She made some grumbling sounds about 'No doubt as soon as I have the kitchen clean you will mess it up again. I know you, there will be bits of car everywhere' but a handful of crumpled pound notes slipped into her hand with instructions to 'get something nice in for supper' quickly put a smile on her face and silenced her grumbles.

On the way there, a few miles from our estate, we passed woods that stretched for several miles. Out of the window I saw the thick clumps of bluebells, couples walking arm in arm, children laughing and dogs of various shapes and sizes scampering in the long grass and something in me longed to be out of that car and to join them. Or maybe it was more that I was looking at a life I wanted.

Feeling my father's gaze on me, I turned my head to meet his eyes.

'You think it looks pretty over there, do you, Cassie?' he asked as though reading my mind. 'Nice place to walk, eh?'

'Yes,' I replied, hoping he would offer to stop the car and take us in there.

He laughed and hearing the undertone of mockery in the sound, prickles of unease ran up my spine. I knew without understanding why that I had given the wrong answer.

He pulled the car onto a verge and switched off the engine. Was he, I wondered, going to open the doors and let us walk there? But he made no move to do so. Instead his hands brushed the top of my head.

'Look then, Cassie. Tell me what you see.'

'Pretty flowers and people looking happy, and dogs ...' I added, for I did not have the words to describe the glitter of pollen spiralling in the air, the shade of the purple-blue flowers I longed to pick, or how, when I glanced up, I saw the white squiggles left behind by a plane on the clear blue sky and I thought of all those people flying high above us.

With the window wound down, the slight breeze swept the sound of the children's laughter towards us. It caused my eyes to be drawn to a little dungaree-clad girl about the same age as myself. Her parents were walking hand in hand, I noticed, while their two dogs, a glossy-coated black Labrador and a tan and white small terrier, ran ahead. It was the smaller dog, which with its tail wagging furiously had pawed furiously at the ground that had made the child laugh. Oh, how I wished then that I was part of a family like that. To be free of our house with its stifling atmosphere and away from my father whose smile I was suddenly wary of.

His voice interrupted my short daydream.

'Proves how little you know,' he said with a chuckle. 'Your grandmother read you the story about Hansel and Gretel, didn't she?'

I nodded my head. Reading us stories was something she did whenever my mother, saying she needed a break, left us there for a day or even a weekend.

'Well, what she didn't tell you was that the story is no fairy tale, it's all true. No doubt she said it was all make-believe, didn't she? But it isn't. Witches don't just live in faraway lands, you know. We have them here as well.'

I tried to say that the witch in my grandmother's book did not come from anywhere near our estate, but taking no notice at my attempt to interrupt him, he put the car into gear and continued talking as he drove.

'I know they were not English witches the children met, Cassie. Oh, don't look so surprised, I know that story. Anyhow, our witches are different – they don't build houses out of sugar for curious children to discover. Oh no, our witches don't live in places like that. So where do you think they live, eh?'

Of course I had no idea so I stayed silent. Part of me thought he was just making it up as he went along. The other part was beginning to feel scared. Could it be true? I wanted him to stop and go back to talking about anything else as long as it wasn't about witches. But I knew better than to tell him that.

'So where do ours live then?' I asked instead, knowing that was the question he wanted to hear.

I was right, for he rewarded me with a smile and a pat on the knee.

'Why our witches live in holes dug deep beneath the ground. And when the sun has gone down and the only light comes from that silvery gleam the moon casts on the world, why that is when they crawl out.'

'But if there are clouds, how do they see in the dark?' I asked, hoping to catch him out for I was still not convinced this was a game he was playing.

'Why they have red eyes that glow in the dark, the same as rats have. And when they come out after sleeping all day, they are very hungry. They look for small creatures to eat. Rabbits and hares, but if they catch a child, a small, plump one like Jimmy here,' he said, gesturing to the back of the car where thankfully my little brother was curled up asleep, 'he would never be seen again. Not even his bones would be found. Oh, don't worry,' he added, noticing no doubt that my face had paled, 'you are a bit too tall for them to fancy. Not to mention rather scrawny as well. No, you'd be safe all right,' a reassurance given more, I am sure, because he did not want a frightened child puking up in his newly cleaned car than any consideration for my feelings.

He said no more for a few moments, just concentrated on taking a cigarette out of its packet and lighting it and I was grateful for the silence. I heard his satisfied sigh as he inhaled deeply, before exhaling a cloud of smoke that flew into my eyes, making me cough. I just hoped he would stop telling stories that were beginning to frighten me. Even though I was still not sure if it was a joke or not, I certainly did not want to hear any more.

'Not frightened you, have I, Cassie?'

'No,' I lied.

'That's my girl! It'd take more than that to scare you, wouldn't it? I know you aren't one of those sniffling little cowards I have no time for.'

A remark I took to be praise.

For the rest of the journey nothing more was said. The sun coming through the screen made me dozy, and like Jimmy, I felt my eyes closing. The next thing I knew we had arrived at the house where the man who sold the cars lived. Jimmy and I were given lemonade and cake by the man's wife, while the two men talked 'business' as my father put it. I heard the man say we were two children to be proud of. A remark that I could see pleased my father.

The car we were to return home in was in much worse condition than the one he had repaired and also much bigger.

'It's a Ford Zephyr,' I was told when I exclaimed at the size of it. 'Going to be a bit of work to get this one through the MOT.'

'But you can do it, Bert, you know you can.'

'Of course! I'm an expert, aren't I?'

'Best in the business!' replied the man and deep complacent masculine laughter rang out.

Once an envelope of money had been tucked away on my father's person and hearty handshakes given, we were back on the road again.

Jimmy did as he always did when he was in a car and fell asleep as soon as we had travelled no more than a few yards. Full of cake and lemonade, it was not long before I too found my eyes closing and they only opened again when the car came to a stop. For a moment, in that stage between sleep and wakefulness, I thought we had arrived home. Then as sleep left me, I saw where he had parked: beside the woods.

Dusk had fallen while I slept, turning the woods into shades of indigo and grey. One of the car windows had refused to shut and through it I could hear the silence. No children's laughter for they had gone home to bed, and no birdsong either. Those bright-eyed little feathered creatures were also in their nests, heads tucked under their wings, already dozing the night away. And I could no longer see the flowers I had longed to pick; their faces were hidden in the dimness.

'You see, Cassie, not everything is pretty all the time.'

He was right: the sunlight leaving had leached away the beauty. In the shadows of approaching night it all appeared secretive, almost menacing. Suddenly I had no difficulty in believing the stories my father had told me of the witches. It was certainly no longer a place I wanted to visit and I just wished he would start the car again.

'Now, Cassie, you know I have a lot of time for you, don't you?' he said. 'You don't annoy me like your brother does. Always scared of something, that moron, but you are different.' And his arm went round my shoulders. 'No, you are special to me all right.'

It was so seldom that I received any praise that I felt a surge of something approaching love on hearing his words, words that wiped out any thought of what had happened on the landing, in my bedroom and in his shed.

'Now, Cassie,' he added, 'I have a test for you, come,' and leaning across me, he opened my door. 'Out you get then, we are going for a little walk, you and your little brother, both. Wake him up.' When I looked in the back and saw Jimmy curled up, his face soft with sleep, I felt a wave of protectiveness.

'He's fast asleep,' I protested, willing my father to leave him where he was.

'Well, I'll wake him up then. Come on, Jimmy, wakey-wakey,' and the little boy sat up, rubbed his eyes and squinted at us with a confused expression.

'Home?' he asked.

'Not yet. We are going for a little walk, so out you get. Your sister will give you a hand.'

As I leaned into the car his arms went trustingly around my neck and I lifted his small, warm body out. I was puzzled: what did my father want with us in the woods? It was growing dark, the sun's leaving had also taken the warmth of the day with it and I found I was shivering slightly. Surely he didn't want to pick flowers? That was not something I could imagine him doing.

'You remember that story I told you, the one we talked about, don't you?' he said and my prickles of unease intensified. 'Bet you forgot to bring any breadcrumbs,' and he laughed before I had a chance to reply.

'Dad, I want to go home,' I pleaded and hearing the shake in my voice, my little brother's hold on my hand tightened.

'Home you will go,' my father said, 'just not yet. Now, concentrate, Cassie, look at the path we are on, because you are going to have to remember it.'

I did as he said and concentrated as hard as I could. What game was he playing now, I wondered, thinking maybe he was just testing me to see if I could lead him and Jimmy back to the car when he had done walking. It's a game, I told myself, I'm sure it's just a game, something I kept repeating to myself with every step we took into the gloom.

'Dad, what are we doing here? It will be dark soon,' I said, trying to push my mounting disquiet aside.

'You'll see.'

It was not only the lack of sunlight that was causing the growing darkness as we went off the main path on to a narrow trail, it was also the denseness of foliage we were walking through. Branches turned into arms that touched my head and slapped my body while their leaves felt like ghostly grasping fingers as they brushed my face and hands. It was not long before I could no longer see the sky through the denseness of the trees.

'Now, that's what I was looking for,' my father suddenly exclaimed as he came to a halt. I glanced around, not understanding what it was he meant. All I could see was a fence at the end of the footpath.

'Here we are then,' he said with a note of triumph in his voice.

Still I could not think what he meant. It was not until we had nearly reached the fence that I saw the stile that gave access to the other side where the continuation of our path cut across the fields. Surely he did not mean to make us climb over the stile and take us into that field, did he? I was sure there would be cows and maybe even a fierce bull. Not a place I wanted to venture into when it was dark. But my father's voice cut into my thoughts and within seconds I understood that what he had planned was far worse than I could have imagined.

'Now, Cassie, what did I say to you earlier? I said you were special, didn't I? And now's your chance to prove it. I'm setting you a test and I don't expect you to disappoint me.'

As I puzzled over what he could mean to my horror a piece of rope was whipped out of his pocket.

'Come here, Jimmy,' and before the little boy had any understanding of what was happening to him, he had been lifted up, placed on the stile with one leg and one hand tied to it. Throughout, although his lips had started to tremble, he remained silent. I knew it was because he was too scared to make a sound. Not even a tiny whimper or a choked-back sob came out of his wide-eyed, frightened face.

'Now, Cassie, here's your test. You can walk out of the forest with me, or I will go and you can stay and untie your brother, then walk back out of the forest with him. The forest is safe until the moon comes out. So you'll have plenty of time. Or, of course, you can leave him here. It's your choice.'

He waited for scarcely a moment until he saw me frantically trying to undo the knots and then he turned his back and strode into the shadows of the woods.

I was frantic; the knots were too tight for my small fingers. I pulled at them but then realising my panic was making them tighter, I took a deep breath and started prising each one apart with my fingers.

'It's just a silly game,' I told the terrified child.

'I want to wee,' was his answer.

'You can very soon,' I replied, hoping that what I was telling him was the truth. A small child, tired and wet as well, would be too much for me to manage.

I could not stop my thoughts turning to those witches due to come out of their holes very soon, their long noses twitching as they searched for prey. How long would it be before the moon came out, I had no idea. Just that thought made tears prickle on my face. Angrily, I brushed them away: they would only cloud my vision and I needed it to untie the knots.

I was aware of the last of the faint trace of the sun's rays disappearing, which meant it would not be long until that silver disc began to rise in the sky. The urge to take to my heels and run after my father became stronger, but looking at my little brother's terrified face, I pushed temptation away and managed to say again that it was only a game.

'Now I know you need to wee, but don't wriggle, it makes the knots tighter.' Obediently he became still.

Because my nails were too short to get into the knots, I bent down and worried them with my teeth as well, until finally I felt them start to loosen. First his arm came free and then his leg.

I hugged him tightly. 'See, all we have to do is follow the path and we will be out of here in no time,' I told him as brightly as I could. For there was another nagging worry: how were we to get home, once we were out of the woods? It would take us hours to walk the distance home.

'Let's just get out,' I told myself. 'I'll think about that then.'

His cold little fingers slipped into mine. 'All right, Cassie?' he said and his fingers tightened. Uncomplainingly, he trudged beside me, a small stalwart figure. I thanked whatever powers had been around me that I had not been cowardly enough to abandon him.

At last we reached the road. Stripped of daylight, it seemed to stretch endlessly into the night. So long and dark, it felt an impossible task and just the thought of that journey home made my legs shake. As I stood there thinking of a plan, bright car lights were suddenly switched on and dazzled me. I heard my father's voice calling us.

'Over here, you two.'

The door was open, he was standing beside it – he had been there all the time, watching us in the dark.

'In you get,' and he lifted my brother into the back seat while I clambered into the front. 'Now, that was an adventure for you two, wasn't it?'

I felt tears of weariness running down my face, but there was another emotion: dismay. How could he have done that to us?

'Don't cry, Cassie. Not when you did so well. You've made me proud of you. I would not have let anything bad happen to you, don't you know that?'

A piece of chocolate was pressed into both our hands, the engine started and warm air from the heater surged around my legs.

'You didn't think I would leave you here, now did you, Cassie?'

Of course I had thought exactly that, but I said, 'No,' although my voice betrayed my hesitancy.

'Good! I was here all the time, you know.'

Years later, when I passed those same woods, I saw through my adult eyes that the haunted forest was not much more than a hundred yards long, and less than that in width.

CHAPTER NINE

It had seemed so vast when I was small. Which was why the man who had left us there, the man who made sure we were so scared we could hardly speak, so much so that Jimmy and I had terrible nightmares for a long time afterwards, had seemed like a saviour to us that night.

And of course that was exactly what the real game had been about.

Chapter Ten

It took several weeks from when I had first met my therapist to bring myself to divulge how, after my father left us in the woods, his demands on me had increased.

'You mean,' she asked when I stumbled over the words, 'the abuse moved from just touching to penetrative sex?'

I felt a sense of relief at her matter-of-fact words; somehow hearing them said so dispassionately made it easier to continue.

'Yes,' I answered softly.

'I've not been able to talk about it before,' I told her, 'not only because I did not want to, but also because over the years I have tried desperately to block much of it out. That first time I must have cried, begged him to stop, and after it was over and he left me there, I can only imagine I huddled under the bedclothes for comfort. I am certain my hands were clasped protectively round my stomach as I tried to ease the pain. For there must have been pain, mustn't there? I was still a little girl. And also blood. Maybe not too much, but enough to terrify the child I was then. I have tried to force my mind back, but each time I do, all I can see is a little girl curled up tightly in a ball in her bed, her face puffy from crying. I can picture that and think of what must have gone on in her prepubescent head. Of course, somehow she would have been blaming herself – that's what children do, isn't it?'

My therapist made no comment. She was, I understood, waiting for me to answer my own questions, the ones I still had no answers for.

'I can remember other times – there were so many of them of course that they have become jumbled up. It's as though I had a scrapbook in my head where I glued disjointed pieces of my childhood, but over the years I forgot to write down either the dates, or the times. I'm still not sure how old I was when my father moved from touching and kissing to using different ways of invading my body. I know it was before I had left junior school, and also it took place during a time I was happy.'

'And you weren't happy before?'

'No, and not for a long time after it either.'

'So what was it that had changed in your life that year to make you happy?'

'I had made a friend, the first real one I ever had. And she was important to me.'

'And have you managed to keep in touch with her since you left school?'

'No, in a way she belongs to another part of my story. I don't want to talk about her today. Not at the same time as the abuse, it somehow taints it. You know even then my father used that friendship to strengthen my trust in him. By doing that, he increased his hold on me. But she is still a good memory and I don't want to tarnish it.'

'I understand. You never want to think of her at the same time as that other part of your childhood.'

'No, I don't.' I was grateful that she appreciated my need for separation.

'Can you explain though, just how he used a friendship to control you. Have you thought that through, Cassie?'

'My mother did not want me to have friends, she expected me to come straight home from school. He, surprisingly, stood up for me, saying it was important for me to have some social life and that as long as my homework was done during the week, I could visit either at weekends or on Fridays after school. "She can catch up with homework over the next couple of days," he pointed out when my mother said sourly that Friday was still a weekday. Later, he even agreed to the occasional sleepover.

'She really hated that he had taken my side against her. She tried to hide her annoyance from him, but behind his back she became even more difficult and critical. It was little things at first that she put down to being busy or forgetful. But I was fully aware that it was all done out of spite. Like my school shirt would not have been washed, which meant I looked more unkempt than usual. The look of malicious glee when I looked for it and it still lay in the dirty washing told me I was being punished. As did the empty bottle of shampoo, when I went to wash my hair. It was my father who, seeing me going to school on a Monday with my shirt all grubby and crumpled, asked my mother why that was.

'He made no comment when she said that I had only myself to blame because I had not put it in the laundry basket and with all the other washing she had to do it was not surprising she had not noticed it was missing. That was such a blatant lie and I can still see the defiant expression on her face, daring us to challenge her.'

'And did you?' my therapist said.

'No, I knew he had his own ways of dealing with her. He just looked at her with a half-smile, told her he had work to do, and left the room.

'He might not have expressed disbelief at her excuses, but later in the day he made his point, one that had far more effect on her than had she been confronted earlier. It was just as she was preparing the evening meal that he came into the kitchen carrying a carrier bag. "This will make sure you always have a clean shirt," he said, handing it to me. And opening it, I found that inside there was not one, but two brand new white cotton shirts.

'"Now look after those, Cassie, and make sure they go in the wash on time, won't you?" He gave me a wink that told me he had not been fooled by my mother's excuses.

'I was fully aware that she was seething with rage at her powerlessness to argue with him, whereas I was almost speechless with gratitude.'

'So,' said my therapist, 'now he was a man who not only had rescued you from witches, but had also stopped you from being in trouble at school as well as allowing you to enjoy your important new friendship?'

'Yes.'

'And you did not want to displease him?'

'No, I didn't,' and I could not meet her eyes as I replied.

And of course I hadn't. I had seen too much of his unpredictable bouts of temper not to know that he could change towards me as well in a nanosecond.

My therapist's soft voice interrupted my thoughts and pulled me back to what it was she wanted us to discuss.

'I think if you try hard, you could remember when it began, Cassie. There's a curtain you have pulled shut over it, the thickest one your mind could produce. I want you to try and draw it back and then tell me what it is you see. Can you do that?'

'I'll try,' I said, without much confidence that I would be able to do it. But I knew I needed to do so and clenching my fists tightly, I sent my mind back to the memories, not just of that day, but the ones leading up to it. However, nothing could lessen the shame that I had lived with for so many years, when in halting sentences I finally managed to tell her how he went about putting into practice what he had really wanted to do with me all along.

He had bided his time for, in his opinion, long enough. When he made his move to rid me of my virginity – not that, at that age, I knew what it meant – any fight I once had was gone. It had taken him months to make sure that he could control me. He used two methods to do it. One was showing what I thought of as kindness, when he supported me against my mother and gave me warm smiles. Then he was the father I had always wanted, someone who would put his arm around my shoulders, lightly brush my cheek and tell me I was his 'special girl'. My emotions betrayed me then, for I would feel the heat of pleasure raise in my cheeks – for that parent who smiled and joked and slipped coins into my pocket so I could buy myself a treat was the one I loved. Those were the times when I forgot the other father, the one with his black moods and his wandering hands that touched me in places I instinctively knew were wrong.

The second method was, when I had not responded to something as he wished me to, he expressed not anger, but disappointment. Then, much to my mother's pleasure, he ignored me until it was I who actively sought his approval.

It was my older brother Ben who mainly saw yet another father, the one whose fierce scowls and raised fists made all of us children quake with fear. His temper was not something I wanted unleashed on me. It was those two emotions, need and fear, that over the months fused together inside my head, until they were impossible to separate. My dependence on him showing his approval had not happened overnight, but once he was sure it was there he was confident he could lead me down the path where I would consent to anything he asked of me. And he was right, for I did.

'Now, you are a big girl, Cassie,' he had said more than once using the same tone of voice he put on when he had handed me over a bag of sweets. 'There is something you are going to learn to like, girls not much older than you do it and they enjoy it. And as your dad, it's my duty to prepare you for being a woman. Do you understand?'

I didn't. He might have told me that I was a big girl, but I did not feel like one.

I was still a little girl, and that was what I wanted to remain. I did not wish to be shown any more glimpses of the adult world. The ones I had been forced to cast my eyes on had only served to convince me that the world was a frightening place. And that prospect made me wary of being alone with him.

It was a Saturday morning when he decided that he had waited long enough.

My mother had gone out visiting her friend Jean, a short, rather plump woman, who with a throaty laugh freely admitted her red hair owed more to a bottle than to nature.

'Little Cass,' she always called me, making me cringe with embarrassment as she ruffled my hair and asked me what I enjoyed most at school.

The two of them were going into town together to shop in the large new supermarket. As Jean had a car, a pale dirty green Morris Minor that my father had found cheaply for her, my mother could do what she called a 'big shop'. They would be gone all morning, I knew, for after filling their trolleys they were bound to visit the store's coffee shop, which sold the little iced cakes made by Mr Kipling that my mother could never resist. She would rather eat them at the store than waste money bringing them home for us all to share, I knew.

Ben was hiding in his room. He had learnt to keep out of our parents' way. For most of the weekend he would scarcely be seen, which was how they liked it. At that age I gave little thought to his isolation, but now I often think of that terrible loneliness he was made to endure. Not even a book to look at, for of course he could not read.

This time my mother had taken Jimmy with her. My father had told her that he was going to be too busy to keep an eye on my younger brother. Even though, useful as I was at looking after him, there should still be an adult in the house.

'It's all right leaving him with Cassie for the odd evening when he's in bed,' he added, 'but not in the daytime when he is into everything. No, Cassie's too young to deal with him if he had an accident.'

'Well, you're going to be here, aren't you? She could always call you if anything happened.'

'I've got to pop out for a bit, so no,' he answered in that tone of voice that stated there was no point in arguing with him. A dirty look in his direction was all she dared do. After much huffing and puffing, which showed she was put out, not to mention her shouting at me to help get Jimmy ready, the two women finally left. The moment the door slammed behind them, I breathed a sigh of relief. For a moment I had thought my mother would say I had to go with them and look after Jimmy while they shopped. But it was still not until I heard the car start up that I relaxed. 'No nagging today,' I thought gleefully. I could sit at the kitchen table and do some drawing. For once I would not hear her voice browbeating me as she told me that I was in the way or that I was wasting my time when I could be doing something useful. Or rather that is, useful for her.

I collected my crayons and a pad of thick white paper, bought from money my father had given me, that were tucked away in my bedroom. I wanted to try my hand at drawing something different. There was a picture in one of my mother's magazines of a blonde-haired woman, who she had said was a famous star, holding a small, fluffy white dog and it was the dog's likeness I wanted to try and capture on paper.

Lost in thought, I didn't hear my father's footsteps as he came quietly through the back door. It was the whiff of his body odour that alerted me to his presence and without turning round I knew he was standing just behind me.

'Just you and me, Cassie, today. We've got the house all to ourselves.'

'Ben's still here,' I said quickly.

'Oh, I hardly think that idiot brother of yours counts, do you? He'll not come out of his room while I'm here, anyhow. So as I said, it's nice, isn't it, just you and me in the house?' His voice was soft and almost murmuring, as his hand stroked the back of my neck. It was not being able to see him without twisting my head round and the dreaded feel of his hand touching me that shattered my little daydream of a peaceful morning. No, I did not think being alone with him in the house was very nice at all. For the man who had come into the kitchen was not the father I wanted to be with.

His hand started to move down my spine and rested just below my waist before sliding down my bottom in circular movements. And suddenly fear flooded my body. It was that special kind of fear when breath is held, legs tremble with sudden weakness and the stomach churns acid that was overwhelming me then. It stifled my voice, stopped me from turning to face him, but it couldn't stop me from hearing every syllable sliding from a mouth, I knew without looking, was twisted into one of his mocking smiles.

I could smell his breath as he leant over me, hot, rancid with last night's beer and stale cigarettes and something else indescribable, a smell that I had come to recognise: the smell of danger.

'Now, what have I been promising you?' and as he spoke his hand moved further down to the hem of my skirt and rested on my knee.

All my instincts were screaming at me to get up, move away from him, and how I wanted to; I wanted to very much, but I was just not capable of it. Instead I did what I had done each time he came into my room: I stayed motionless and silent. 'If I did not move then he would stop, wouldn't he?' were the words of the mantra I silently chanted, but he never had.

'You're going to be a good girl, Cassie, aren't you?' he said and, pulling me up, he half carried, half pushed me, to the foot of the stairs.

When I got to that part I just looked at my therapist helplessly.

'I can't,' I said. 'I know what he did, I just don't want to remember it. Do you know what question comes into my mind when I think of him then? Just how old was I when he looked into the future and planned how he could turn me, his daughter, into a toy? A little girl doll just for him to take out and play with whenever he wanted. Was it the moment I was born, all pink and defenceless, and he heard the doctor say, "Congratulations, it's a girl"? I think it was.'

It was hearing myself articulate that belief with such conviction that made me for the first time since I had set foot in that office break down. This time it was not a little moisture in my eyes, which could be wiped quickly away with a tissue from the box she kept so near at hand, or an emotion that might be calmed by inhaling nicotine, but great heaving sobs, where tears ran down my face and dripped from my nose and I was just too distressed to reach for the means to mop them up.

If that was the first time I had lost control of my emotions, it was also the first time my therapist touched me. As my body heaved with those wracking, anguished cries, she knelt by my side and placed an arm around my shoulder.

'It's good to cry, Cassie,' she said and placed a wad of tissues in my hand.

'I think we both need some strong coffee,' and within seconds the comforting aroma of the fresh brew filled her office. She waited until my sobs had subsided then placed a cup of steaming coffee and the obligatory ashtray in front of me. Gratefully, I dived into my handbag in search of the sedatives in cigarette form.

It was only when I had lit one and took my first deep inhalation that she spoke again.

'Cassie, would you rather we left talking about your father until another day?'

'No,' I said adamantly, 'I feel as if I am finally releasing all that poison that has been in my head for so long. It's a bit like lancing a boil, isn't it? Hurts like hell while it's being done and afterwards, though soon the pain is gone and we feel better. That's what I want to believe anyway.

'It's just hard to take in that we are not talking about a stranger or even a man my mother married, like a stepfather or a boyfriend, but this man is the one who fathered me. You know, I was christened in church. Surely then he promised to care for me? And as a child I believed he did. I really thought he loved me. How could he? How could any father? And do you know the worst thing?'

'No, Cassie, tell me what you think it is.'

'I believed that. Believed he cared for me, believed I really was special to him, even after everything that happened. I still carried on believing it, because I wanted to. So what does that make me?'

'Normal,' she said softly. 'It makes you normal, Cassie. All children want is not just to be loved, but to love in return. Love is the strongest emotion. I think we are born with that inside us. Its opposite, hate, is an emotion that has to be learnt. What you have to start believing is that there was nothing wrong with you then, and there is nothing at all wrong with you now. You have reacted normally to an abnormal situation, one you have never let yourself come to terms with. And once you accept that, your world, that you feel trapped in, will change forever. You've built walls made of guilt, walls that keep everyone out. And they will, if you want them to, and I believe you do, come down, brick by brick.'

She was right: I did want them to come down. It was just that I had never thought it possible. I also knew that the only way it was going to happen was if I allowed myself to trust her, and opened up to her completely. If I was to progress there must be no more holding back. My mind made up, I mentally drew back my shoulders, and drawing on my cigarette as deeply as I could, I proceeded to tell her about the rest of what happened that day. I could see those images so clearly it was as though I was describing a film where my father and I were the only characters in it, and I had just pressed the replay button. As I saw it unfolding, I was whirled back several decades in time until I was facing my younger self.

Dressed in a green and white checked dress, a skimpy blue jumper pulled over it for warmth, I'm at the top of the stairs. The door of my room is only inches from my face, and I am looking up at my father imploringly.

'No, Dad,' I am saying. 'Please don't, I don't want to go in there.'

It's a sentence I am repeating because I know that once we enter my bedroom, something dreadful is going to happen.

'Cassie, now stop your nonsense. I'm not going to hurt you,' and a finger, hard and bony, is pressing into my back. It gives me one hard impatient prod and I am staggering through the doorway into my bedroom.

'Now, a little lie down will do you good,' he says, 'so under the covers with you,' and he is lifting the bedspread, motioning me to crawl under. 'Come on, Cassie, in you get. Time for a cuddle, I know you like them.' His voice is both wheedling and firm. My willpower to resist his commands is vanishing and so I reluctantly do as he says.

The bed sags, he is lying behind me. I can feel the pressure of his arm wrapping around my body and he draws me tightly into his chest. A hand moves over me. I can feel its heat through my clothes. My eyes are squeezed shut but behind the lids I see that huge black spider. It's crawling all over me, now it's reached my tummy. I can feel my father's breath on my neck, hear it growing deeper and harsher. And still I am repeating my mantra, 'Stay still, Cassie. Don't talk, don't move, he'll stop soon.' But it's ceasing to calm me and I am trying to wriggle away. Now his arm is no longer holding me gently but pinning me down, his voice rumbling in my ear, 'For God's sake, stay still, will you, Cassie!' and now it's the voice of the angry father, the one who frightens me. At its sound my muscles stiffen and I am lying motionless. The spider is moving down my body, down to my skirt; it's underneath it, moving up to my knickers. Now it changes back into a hand, one that yanks my knickers right down to my ankles.

My father's body is moving. He is no longer lying beside me but crouching over my small frame so that he is blocking out the light. There is something hard prodding me. I attempt to kick out, but I can't – my knickers are binding my ankles together. Whimpering with fear, I want him to stop; I don't like what is happening. This is worse than all the other times. I want to go downstairs, but any sounds I make are being muffled as he presses my head into the pillow. My jumper is being pulled up. I feel his impatience when he touches my dress underneath it, then that too is being pushed up around my neck. I feel cold air on my back. His hands are now everywhere, stroking, kneading, going in between my legs, rubbing that soft place between them and then a finger is sliding inside me.

This was worse, much worse, than anything he had done before. For now there is no gentleness in any of his actions. I am trying to cry out again, trying to say I don't like it, but the pressure against my neck silences me.

'Lie still, I won't hurt you, Cassie,' he murmurs and his voice has gone back to being the one belonging to the nice father. But still I am not reassured. He is tugging off my knickers, pulling them over my feet, but before I can move my legs, he is between them, forcing them wide apart. That hard thing is being pushed between my splayed legs; in and out it is going, rubbing the tops of my thighs.

'Now, Cassie, that's not hurting you, is it?' And still it's the nice voice. 'Now nod your head for me, if you are going to promise to behave.'

He'll stop then, won't he, if I nod? So I'm doing that. I can hear him chuckling – it's not a sound I like. 'Good girl,' he is saying and I feel a pillow slipping under my bottom, causing my middle part to rise higher: he is above me again. I peek up through my eyelashes but quickly close them firmly shut. His face is looking different, flushed and swollen; it scares me even more, I don't want to see it.

I know he is holding that hard thing, stroking it. I can hear it, I feel it against my soft place, rubbing there; and then he pushes hard and it's inside me. I am pinned by it to the bed. It's hurting, I want to cry out; a hand goes over my mouth. 'Shush,' he says. I am clenching my fists and I am still motionless, my eyes tightly shut, but this time there is no mantra running through my head. Instead I am asking myself, 'Why is he doing this to me, what is it I have done?'

Now his body is shuddering. He is crying out. Something wet and sticky is spurting out of the hard thing; it's on my legs. 'Oh good girl, good girl, Cassie!' he is saying, but I don't feel good.

He is rolling off me, his arm still holding my body.

'Now tell me you didn't like that,' he says.

But I cannot speak; I just want to cry.

'I do this because I love you, Cassie. That's what love is,' he whispers in my ear. 'It's what daddies do with their little girls,' he explains. 'Every little girl does it. But it's a secret, and you must not talk about it. It means you love me and you are my own special little girl. You want me to love you, don't you?'

But this time I cannot say yes. He is climbing out of the bed, pulling on his trousers now. He takes some coins out of his pocket. 'Buy yourself some sweets next time you go to the shops,' he is saying and still I cannot talk.

I am so confused: he has frightened me, hurt me, but now his voice is all warm again and I want to ask why, if every little girl does this, why must I not talk? But I remain silent.

His footsteps are on the stairs; I am getting out of bed. My stomach is hurting and there is a dull pain down there. I am pulling on my clothes, my legs are wobbling, but I want to go to the bathroom – I need to wee and I want to wipe that stickiness off me. I am sitting on the toilet, wiping myself, wiping away the stickiness, and then I am looking at the paper in horror: it is streaked with blood.

The film fast forwards until I see the child I once was back in her room. She's sitting on the bed, arms around her knees. She can hear the rain, not the light drizzle of earlier, but great gushes, falling from the sky. She raises her head, looks towards the window and sees her reflection: a girl with a million tears streaming down her face.

That was the moment when the child I could have grown up to be, a child full of love and trust, turned into a silvery wraith and flew from my body – for he had killed her that day.

Chapter Eleven

'Did you have no one you could go to for help?' my therapist asked.

I thought then of what had happened that one time when I had.

'I thought I did,' I said. 'And I went to her. My friend was still in my life and we were at that age when best friends just didn't keep secrets from each other. But even though I was a child, I knew I could never tell her what was happening in my home. In a way, that made me feel even more alone.'

'And what happened?'

'It made everything far worse. That was when I learnt that some adults blame children for what their fathers have done. They don't want to hear about it, and even worse, they are almost disgusted by us, for daring to talk about it; resent us for involving them and want the problem to disappear. And in my case, it was me who was the problem. That was really a horrible time for me.'

'It must have been,' she said gently. 'Cassie, would you rather leave talking about this until the next time you come?' Then seeing more tears were threatening to flow, she said,

'Maybe we need to change the subject to something that is not so upsetting. You have opened up a lot today, and I know it can't be easy for you.'

'Yes, I'd prefer that.'

'I know you said you did not want to talk about your friend on the same day as you have talked about the abuse, but even though you say that your friend went out of your life, she is still a good memory?'

'Yes, she is.'

'And it is important to remember good things even though often that is difficult. You see, Cassie, the three things we have lodged the most firmly in our minds are the memories of loss, fear and humilation. They can override the happy ones and it is important not to let them. Do you understand that?'

'Yes, I think so,' I said hesitatingly.

'Well, let's talk a little about her, shall we?'

And after all the years that had passed I still found myself smiling at those images of the bittersweet times I had spent with Sophia. Memories that, until I had therapy, I had suppressed, for until then I had no one to share them with. And even now as I did then, I wonder what the reasons were for what happened at the end of my knowing her.

I had heard Sophia's name and knew a little about her, even before we met. In fact the whole school was curious about her ever since it had been announced that a new pupil was joining our school and would be in our class. It was not our teacher who told us that, but the Headmistress during morning assembly.

The new girl's parents had just moved into the area and ours was the school they wanted their daughter to attend, she had informed us with a certain amount of pride in her voice. At this we all waited for what else she was going to say. For although it was unusual for a new girl to join us in mid-term, that on its own did not usually warrant our Headmistress feeling the need to announce it to the whole school.

She went on to tell us that the girl, whose name she told us was Sophia Pearson, had Albinism.

'Hands up if anyone here knows what that means,' she said, and we all glanced at each other to see if anyone knew, but not one hand was raised. Instead there was complete silence as we all waited expectantly.

'It means,' she had said, and here she paused briefly, no doubt searching for the right words to explain it as simply as she could to a large group of children, all of differing ages but all under the age of twelve. 'Well, it's a word that describes someone who has very pale hair and skin. Because of that, they have to be very careful in the sun.'

A red-haired girl's hand shot up.

'Yes, Connie?'

'Well, Miss, I always have to use sun cream on warm days or I burn. So do you mean I am the same?'

'No, you are just sun sensitive because of your fair colouring. People with Albinism cannot go outside on a very hot day unless they are wearing a really strong sunblock. They can also have very poor eyesight, which unfortunately, Sophia has. And that is the main reason I am speaking to you all today. I want you all to look out for her and be extra careful not to bump into her or accidentally trip her up.

'She will have a desk at the front of the class, but it will need to be turned away from the window so that the light does not get into her eyes. And when she goes outside she has to wear dark glasses. But if it's a very hot day, then she will stay inside.

'Now, will you all promise me that you will make her welcome?'

'Yes, Miss,' we chorused before being summarily dismissed.

Of course much of the chatter once we were out of assembly was about the new arrival. We were all curious as to what she would look like, this little girl who was so pale she could not venture out into the sunlight.

The following day Sophia arrived. I saw a diminutive figure with curly white hair and skin, which untouched by the sun, was even paler than Connie's. Blue-rimmed glasses framed her eyes and even from where I sat, I could see the lenses were not just extremely thick, but tinted as well. She seemed, I thought, uncommonly poised for one entering a classroom full of strangers. She must have been aware that with her hair and thick glasses, she was to receive curious glances, but if she noticed any, they had little effect on her composure. The teacher introduced her before indicating where her desk was, and, taking neat little steps, Sophia walked to it and took her seat.

CHAPTER ELEVEN

When the bell rang announcing it was break time, I noticed her swap her classroom glasses for sun ones, so dark it was impossible to see her eyes through them. Once they were firmly on her nose, she stood up and followed us out into the corridor. There was quite an assurance about her, almost a remoteness, which stopped anyone approaching her. I watched out of the corner of my eye as she walked along, her head bent slightly forward so I could see the pink of her scalp where her hair parted. When she reached the doors leading to the playground I could tell her eyes were fixed more on the ground than on her classmates. This was not, as I came to learn, out of shyness, but a fear of tripping over an outstretched leg, a stray satchel or a chair pushed carelessly in her way.

Once she reached the playground she stood quite close to the teacher and I saw them exchanging words before she turned and stood watching a group of girls playing with a skipping rope. No doubt mindful of the Head's instructions to make the new girl feel welcome, one of the girls from the group walked over to her. I could not hear what was being said, but guessed it was an invitation for her to join them. Sophia smiled, shook her head and the teacher said something, which I was told later was to let the group know it was not out of unfriendliness that Sophia had refused to play, but because with her bad eyesight, it was just too risky.

Once my classmates realised she could not join in their games, they stopped trying to include her. Over the next few days it was as though a cloak of invisibility had been draped over her shoulders. I felt sorry for her then. I knew what it was like not to be included, even if the reason the children avoided me was totally different. First, I was an unkempt child from the roughest part of the council estate. Second, if that alone did not stop their parents from wanting their children to mix with me, the appearance of my older brother Ben did. For some inexplicable reason, looking as different as he did was simply not acceptable to young children or their parents.

It was Sophia who, at the beginning of her second week at our school, approached me. Up close, I saw her skin was not white as I had first thought, but a delicate pink which reminded me of the inside of the conch shell my grandmother had sitting on her sideboard.

'Cassie,' she asked, 'why are you not playing with the other girls?'

'Maybe,' I thought, 'she is wondering if I too have bad eyesight or maybe she has heard the whispers, knew the reason, and paid little heed to it.'

'They don't ask me,' I said simply and instead of displaying any curiosity as to why, she just said, 'Shall we sit together at lunch then?' And I am sure in that moment my face was just one big smile of gratitude. That was the beginning of a friendship that ended all too briefly but it has stayed in my mind for all these years.

When the bell rang announcing it was lunchtime, I moved over to Sophia's desk and watched as she took off those thick glasses and put them meticulously into their case. It was then that I saw not only her hair, but her lashes and brows were white as well. Without them, her face had a naked, vulnerable look that made me feel suddenly protective of her. As she placed the glasses case in her bag before taking out her dark sunglasses, I saw it was her fingers, not her eyes, which looked for them; her head had remained still. I think it was at that moment I realised that without those thick lenses, her world would be at most a blur of indistinct shapes and shadows.

It did not take long for us not only to sit together at lunch but to stand chatting during our breaks and by the end of the week we were waiting for each other in the playground each morning so that we could walk into assembly together.

I saw the teachers watching us, sensed they did not approve of this sudden new friendship, but without me doing something wrong, there was little they could say. Especially as Sophia had introduced me to her mother, Mrs Pearson, who with her long, shiny dark hair, colourful clothes and jangling bracelets bore little resemblance to the other women waiting for their children. She in turn seemed not only unfazed by my shabby appearance, but by Ben as well. Seeing us all standing together, he, with Jimmy walking sheepishly behind him, had ambled over to where we were.

'Hello,' Mrs Pearson said, bestowing a wide friendly smile on them both. 'Cassie, are these your two brothers? Sophia told me they were at this school as well.'

'Yes,' I replied, wondering what else had been said about Ben. But the real question that had been running through my head the moment I had spotted him walking towards us was would Mrs Pearson still want her daughter and me to be friends when she met him?

'Well then, I think you had better introduce me to them, hadn't you?'

I gulped. People might have said that Jimmy was cute, but no one I had met so far had shown any desire to meet Ben.

'This is my little brother, Jimmy,' I managed to say and at the sound of his name a cheeky grin appeared on my younger brother's round face. 'And this is Ben,' I added, my fingers mentally crossed that he would not utter one of his strange keening sounds as he did both when either nervous or upset. But I need not have worried. Ben even managed to vocalise 'Hello' and gave her one of his goofy smiles. She in turn gave no hint of being the least bit perturbed by him.

'Well, it's very nice to meet you both,' she replied and another wide smile was aimed in their direction.

'Is your mother coming to fetch you, Cassie?' she then asked, glancing around the playground.

'No,' I answered, not mentioning this was not something my mother had ever done for any of us. 'It's not far, and anyhow, we all walk back together.'

'Well, I'm sure Ben takes care of you. It must be nice to have a big brother,' she said before walking away, her arm gently resting on Sophia's shoulder.

'I like her,' said Jimmy as soon as Sophia and her mother were out of earshot.

'I do too,' echoed Ben.

'Yes,' I thought, 'I do as well,' for I had noticed the little squeeze she had given Ben's arm as she left, and seen him blush with pleasure at it. Just a small kindness that made his day, and I liked her so much for it.

It was no more than a week after I had met Sophia's mother than I was handed a note to give to my own mother.

'It's an invitation for you to come to tea on Friday,' Sophia told me. 'My mother will drive you home afterwards, so yours does not have to worry about how you will get back. Oh, say you'll come, Cassie,' and with each word she spoke the pink of her face deepened. Holding the envelope tightly in my hand, I was momentarily speechless. 'You do want to come, don't you, Cassie?' she added, obviously mistaking my silence for unwillingness.

'Of course I do,' I said, clutching the envelope to my chest before placing it carefully in my satchel. I could hardly have told her that it was the surprise of being given an invitation that had robbed me of my speech. I did not want to admit it was the first time ever that I had been invited by another pupil's mother to visit their house.

'She'll meet us here after school,' Sophia continued happily. 'Oh, Cassie, it will be so nice to have you over.'

A string of questions followed. 'Did I like dolls?' A question I gave an enthusiast 'yes' to. 'And snakes and ladders?' I guessed that was a game, but I had no idea what it was. Seeing that I looked puzzled, she grinned, took my hand and said, 'Don't worry, Cassie, I'll show you how to play. It's easy and such fun!' Then she listed all the other board games she had at her disposal: Monopoly, dominoes and Scrabble, none of which I had heard of.

'My grandmother taught me how to play snap,' I volunteered, wanting to make some contribution to our conversation.

'Well then, I'll show you heaps of new ones,' and with that I suddenly realised she was just as excited as I was at the invitation: in having a new friend over to her house.

For the rest of the day, as I thought of that letter tucked safely away in my satchel, I felt a warm glow. That was until I got home.

'No.'

My mother read the letter and handed it to my father for inspection with a sneer. 'You are not going to a house where I don't know the people. Anyhow, you have your chores to do here or were you forgetting them?'

'Oh, let her go, Liz. Be nice for her to have friends,' said my father unexpectedly. 'And have you seen their address? Really swanky area that! Looks like our little Cassie is going up in the world. Be sure and tell them I'm good with cars,' he added with a wink.

'Anyhow,' he said, turning to my mother, 'one less mouth to feed on Friday, isn't it?' A remark I could see did little to wipe the disgruntled expression off her face.

On seeing it, he turned to me: 'Now, one good turn deserves another, don't it, Cassie? So you look after Jimmy on Saturday night and I'll take your mother down the pub for a couple. Will you do that?'

'Yes, Dad,' I agreed willingly. I could see that his suggestion had mollified my mother slightly, which was a relief. I did not need her bad temper and anger with me for the next three days.

The following morning, I awoke to bright sunlight and thought immediately of Sophia. She could not stay outside if the sun became too strong. Would she even be waiting for me in the playground?

She wasn't, and my heart sank. I thought then that maybe she could not even attend school, but no, she was waiting for me inside. Even the rays of the early morning sun were too hot for her. By mid-morning our classroom felt hot and stuffy, my clothes were sticking to my back and the back of my neck was damp. Outside the sun was beating down relentlessly and I longed to be sitting somewhere cool instead of in the hot classroom.

Once the bell announcing break time rang, Sophia told me that she would have to remain in the classroom: 'The sun is just too strong today,' she said and I heard a tinge of unhappiness in her voice. She must have wanted to be able to join in with the other children and not always have to remember to swap her glasses and put on that thick sunscreen that made her even hotter.

I asked the teacher if I could stay with her, a request that was firmly denied: 'No, Cassie, you need fresh air so out to the playground with the others you go. I'm sure Sophia will not disappear while you are outside.' By the firmness in her voice

I knew there was no point in arguing so dragging my feet to show my displeasure, I reluctantly followed my classmates out into the playground.

For the rest of that week the heat showed no sign of abating. We were having what the newspaper headlines described as a 'heatwave', which meant I saw less of Sophia than usual. During our breaks she was restricted to staying in the classroom while I stood outside feeling the empty space beside me.

'It takes forever to put the cream on every bit of my skin that the sun can reach,' she told me. 'Mummy puts it on every morning, but it soon rubs off. I have a big sunhat but I don't want to wear it at school – I look enough of a freak already.'

'No, you don't,' I insisted loyally.

She smiled and patted my arm.

'I know that the Head gave everyone a talk. She probably told you all to be nice to me. And that is because of the way I look, not because of my eyesight. One day Mummy says I am going to go to a school where everyone is the same as me.'

'What? Everyone there has white hair?'

'No, where everyone's eyes don't work as well as yours do.'

At this I felt a little flutter of dread: I did not want Sophia going to another school. Sensing this, she just said, 'Oh, it won't be for ages, Cassie,' and reassured, I pushed that thought to the back of my mind.

The anticipated Friday arrived. Outside, the other children seemed oblivious to the heat. Unlike mine, all the other girls' dresses still looked clean and crisp. I longed to take off my cardigan – it was hot and scratchy – but I was far too conscious of a tear in my dress just under the arm. The night before, I had asked my mother if it could be mended. Her reply was the one I expected. 'Not got time,' she had said and I sensed that again she was enjoying my discomfort.

I wanted Sophia's mother to approve of me. She always sent her daughter off to school looking squeaky clean and tidy – there was never a dirty mark or a rip on Sophia's clothes. Whatever her thoughts might have been, when she saw me, hot and dishevelled, walking towards her, Mrs Pearson hid them with one of her warm smiles.

'Come on, girls,' she enthused, 'let's get in the car.'

'You sit in the front, Cassie,' Sophia told me. 'You can see more and I'm in it every day.'

'It's the new Mini,' Mrs Pearson explained once I had climbed in and told her I had never seen a car like it. 'It's lots of fun.'

And with its bright yellow exterior, it was, I thought, the prettiest car I had ever seen. Much nicer then the big old Fords my father repaired.

'Some music, I think, girls,' said Mrs Pearson as she drove off and to my astonishment I watched wide-eyed as, with what seemed like a few effortless flicks of her hand, she loaded several cassettes into a machine tucked just under the dashboard. 'It's called an eight-track, Cassie,' she said laughingly when she saw the surprise on my face. 'Usually they are put in the big posh cars like Bentleys, but I decided my Mini was as good as them and deserved one too. Now, what sort of music do you like?'

This was a question she quickly saw I had no answer to. Although our radio blared out a lot during the daytime, it was seldom tuned into a music programme. Neither of my parents had ever expressed any interest in it.

'Well, here's my favourite. Let's give it a go and see if you like it,' she said, pressing a button, and a raspy male voice suddenly filled the car, singing about a woman called 'Maggie May'.

'Rod Stewart,' she told me. 'I simply love him.'

Another button was pressed and a gush of cool air fell on my face.

'It's air conditioning,' she answered when I asked where it was coming from. 'I had that added as well – I can't stand being too hot or too cold for that matter. The Americans have it right, they even have it in their homes.'

'Wish we had it at school,' I said, thinking of the clammy classroom I had spent much of the day in. I leant back in my seat enjoying both the feel of the coolness and the sound of the music and thinking this was the perfect start to my visit.

I felt a jolt of disappointment when within a short space of time we pulled into the driveway that led up to the house. Much as I was looking forward to seeing where Sophia lived, I was enjoying the car journey so much that I would have been happy had it lasted longer.

The driveway ended in front of a rambling grey stone house with long oblong windows that stood behind a large expanse of green lawn, shadowed by the foliage of several thickly leaved trees. I wondered what my father would say – it was far grander than the square redbrick ones about which he complained so vociferously.

'I expect you girls need a cold drink now,' Mrs Pearson said as she led us through a black and white tiled hallway down a wooden-floored corridor and into a large kitchen. Painted a pale yellow with pine cupboards, there was a long table with a matching bench covered in thick red cushions that dominated. It was far smarter than any sitting room I had ever been in.

'That's where we eat most of the time,' said Mrs Pearson, noticing me looking at it. 'It means I don't have to leave my guests while I'm cooking.' My eyes were darting all around the room and I saw above my head a large assortment of saucepans hanging from a circular rack and then I noticed a row of pots filled with leafy green plants lining the window sill.

'My herbs,' Mrs Pearson explained when she saw they had caught my eye. 'I like being able to pick them fresh and toss them into my cooking.' But the word 'herbs' was another word I did not understand: salt and pepper was used in our house and sometimes tomato ketchup or a dark sauce out of a jar and just occasionally mustard, but I could not imagine my mother putting little green leaves into anything she cooked.

'Sophia, take Cassie into the conservatory, and I'll bring us something to eat,' Mrs Pearson said brightly, after she had filled two tumblers with lemonade. No doubt she had realised that ever since I had climbed into her car, she might just as well have been speaking a foreign language. Picking up our drinks, I followed Sophia into a room made of glass. Tubs of flowers I had never seen inside before were placed at one end, blinds covered a large section of the windows and in front of them were white armchairs, which I was told when I asked were made of wicker. The concept of a conservatory was another first for me and I wondered what else I was going to find in Sophia's home that I had no previous knowledge of.

Through the windows I could see that the garden was full of flowers and shrubs and at the far end were several apple trees. 'I like that plant best,' said Sophia, pointing to a dark green shrub with small purple buds that I thought the least attractive one.

'My favourite also,' said her mother as she brought in a tray with sandwiches and cake for us. 'See those dark purple buds on it? In another few weeks they will be in full bloom and then we'll have a swarm of butterflies hovering all around it. I call it my butterfly tree.'

She sat with us while we ate our sandwiches and after placing large slices of coffee cake on our plates, she told me that she would leave me in Sophia's hands.

'I'm sure she will want to show you her room,' she added brightly. Then, leaving a beautiful glass jug of more lemonade, 'homemade', as she told me, she left us to our own devices.

And she was right. As soon as the last crumbs of cake had been swallowed Sophia was up on her feet, telling me I had to see her doll's house. Needing no persuasion, I followed her up a wide staircase carpeted in a deep blue. A collection of family photos and a couple of large landscape paintings set in plain gilded frames caught my eye and then we were at the top of the stairs. Turning left, we walked past a couple of doors before Sophia opened the one leading into her room. If everything in the house was bigger and prettier than anything in ours, then her bedroom was even more so. It looked twice the size of my room and that of my parents put together.

There were duck egg blue walls, cream carpeting and white fitted full-length cupboards with round gilt handles. She had a whole wardrobe just for herself, I realised, and contrasted it to my bedroom with its small dark brown chest of drawers and a hook on the back of the door to hang my sparse collection of clothes on. I took in the rest of the room: her bed, with a deep pink headboard, was covered in a brightly coloured patchwork quilt and over the windows hung floor-length curtains of a blue so dark they were almost black, tied back by thick twined gold-coloured ropes.

But it was not just the furniture making my mouth gape open but the sight of the doll's house standing on a low square table. I had once seen one in a shop window and my hands had twitched with wanting to touch it, but this … If I had the words I would have said it was magical, a kingdom in miniature. Painted a soft cream with a green roof, it was two storeys high.

'Look, Cassie,' Sophia said and, leaning over my shoulder, she pressed a switch and lights came on, illuminating every room. Inside was a whole family: two children, a dark-haired boy and beside him a girl doll dressed in a pink and white gingham dress, were in one of the bedrooms, which I saw was furnished almost exactly the same as Sophia's. There were two more bedrooms and a bathroom upstairs, while downstairs was a kitchen, again very similar to the one I had just seen, and a sitting room where two adult dolls stood.

I was completely entranced by it, as I was by the collection of Barbie dolls that we spent most of the afternoon dressing and undressing.

I could never invite Sophia to visit me, I thought then. And surely a return invitation would be expected? That thought brought pictures of our house: my bedroom, with its sagging single bed covered in a worn grey blanket my grandfather had been given when he fought in the war, my mother's sour face and my father wearing his dirty work clothes, stomping into the kitchen rose in my mind.

But I need not have worried. Sophia's mother was, I am sure, only too aware of what our home must be like and was most probably as reluctant to have her daughter visit as I was to ask her. When she drove me back after my visits, she must have noticed the state of the patch of garden in front of the house and the unwashed net curtains hanging at the windows. No doubt she had also seen that neither my clothes nor my brothers' were always clean and by the end of the week my hair needed washing. She might be pleased that Sophia had a friend but that did not mean she wanted her daughter spending time with my family. Perhaps she sensed my concern because she always gave me another invitation when I left. Gradually I accepted that it was understood that Sophia was never going to come to our house. Oh, the mothers met occasionally when mine opened the door to me after a visit. She had even invited Mrs Pearson in a couple of times, only to receive an excuse of 'Have to get back' or 'I left dinner on' or something my mother said she felt was equally unconvincing. However, Mrs Pearson seemed to genuinely like me. In fact, so welcome did she make me feel, I quickly began to see the rambling grey stone house as my second home.

As well as playing with dolls and moving the tiny figures around the doll's house, Sophia was the one keen on board games and took pleasure in teaching me the rules. Sometimes we played them in her room, but more often than not, we commandeered the kitchen table, which I liked. Mrs Pearson busied herself with cooking but that did not stop her chattering to us as she did. I was beginning to allow myself to feel part of the family.

I enjoyed watching Mrs Pearson cook, seeing her hands covered in flour when she baked and asked us about school and what we had done that day. When it was a cake she had made, Sophia and I were given the bowl to lick out. And our fingers busily wiped up little dollops of the sweet mixture before we placed them in our mouths. My grandmother was the only other person who had allowed me to do that. Even if my mother had baked a cake instead of buying them from the supermarket, I knew she would not have permitted this. Everything in their home was so different to ours: there I was included in conversation, asked questions and had my answers listened to, as though they mattered.

As well as board games and dressing-up dolls, there was another game we played as so many children do: 'What did we want to be when we were grown up?' Amidst spasms of giggles we named the most absurd ones we could think of. Astronaut was one I thought of, not that I had a very clear idea of what that meant, and mountaineer was one that, spluttering with laughter, Sophia came up with. It was after I had been visiting for several weeks that she said more seriously that what she really wanted to be was a doctor, an admission I noticed produced a slight frown on Mrs Pearson's face.

Some time after we played that game, Sophia told me she did not want to talk any more about what she would do when we were grown-ups.

'Why not?' I asked, for it was a game I enjoyed.

'It's no good, Cassie, I'm never going to be a doctor,' she said sadly. 'The eye specialist told Mummy my eyes will never get better; in fact, they are very likely to get worse. I think one day all I will be able to see will be blackness. Mummy said it will never get as bad as that, but I'm scared it will. I wanted a bicycle for my birthday, but I can't have one – it's too dangerous. So I'll never be able to drive a car either, or play tennis or any other sport.

'It was when she heard us talking about what we want to be when we grow up that made her sit down and explain this to me. I don't think she wanted me to know yet, but I suppose I always have really – I mean, I know I can't see like you can.'

It was so seldom that Sophia ever mentioned her restricted sight that I did not know what to say. She had not sounded like a little girl when she told me all that but more like an adult. Children can paint any picture of their future they want. They can dream of careers that they are completely unsuited for as it's only pretend and deep down they are aware of it. But Sophia, at an age when she was still playing with dolls, had to push those dreams aside and look at the reality of what she was going to be capable of in the future. So like me, she too had been given a glimpse of the adult world that she would one day be part of.

Sophia only talked about her eyesight to me one more time; it was the time that I lost her.

As our friendship deepened, I realised even then that there was a part of her that she kept tucked away. Because of her white hair and dark glasses she knew that she attracted glances even in the road and was just as wary as I was of being mocked. The Headmistress might have made sure that bullying did not happen, but because Sophia was unable to take part in any sport or join in the playground games, she was never going to be accepted by her peers. Certainly I never saw any invites to parties coming her way either.

I was used to not being accepted, but I wondered if she was. She never talked about what her previous school had been like or if, when they moved, she had left any friends behind. Sensing this was not something she wanted to talk about, I never asked. I was happy, in the selfish way young children can be, that she only had me for company. We had our own games and I told myself that neither of us needed other children's company. We squealed with delight when we played snap and concentrated quietly when it was Scrabble. Sophia was much better at it than me but because of that game my spelling began to improve. Dominoes were another one I liked but my favourite was always Monopoly – I just loved bidding and piling up the properties I bought. And I also liked the feel that it was just the three of us in the house. No brothers getting in my way, and no father in the kitchen.

Sophia did have a father, but unlike mine, he worked in an office somewhere in the City and mostly returned home after I had left. On the odd occasion when I met him, I saw a tall man with brown hair shot through with grey and bright blue eyes. I felt uncomfortable around him, maybe because with his dark suit and white shirt, he was so much smarter than my father. Or perhaps I had already grown distrustful of men in general. Whichever it was, I just thought then that he had appraised my clothes, heard my local accent and did not approve of me. The result of those thoughts was that each time we met, I was completely tongue-tied. And I was soon aware that my sleepovers seemed to be arranged when either he was working late or away on business.

Staying the night at Sophia's house was something I simply loved. My bed, with its cool ironed cotton sheets and soft pillows, was so pretty and smelt of cleanness and fresh air.

CHAPTER ELEVEN

The first time I stayed over, I was surprised when Mrs Pearson came into our room.

'Lights going out now, girls, so do either of you need to go to the bathroom?'

'No,' we both said in unison.

'Good, then I don't expect to hear your door opening in the next few minutes, do I?' A question that received giggles as an answer. Leaning over Sophia's bed, she gently removed her daughter's glasses and placed them on the bedside table before bending down and kissing her.

'Love you, little one,' she said.

'Love you too, Mummy.'

The bedclothes were pulled up over Sophia's shoulders before she came over to my bed.

'Hope you sleep well too, Cassie,' and with that she bent down and kissed me on the cheek. I inhaled her perfume and felt her hair brush my face and I so wanted to do as Cassie had, to throw my arms around her neck and be held for a moment, but this was something I sensed that I should not do.

I felt the covers being tucked in around me, heard the click of the light switch and the rustle of her skirt as Mrs Pearson left. Then, feeling safe in Sophia's room, I turned over contentedly and fell into a deep, dreamless sleep.

'Yes, I can see how that is a nice memory, Cassie,' my therapist said.

'It is,' I agreed, smiling at her.

I could sense a question hanging in the air because something must have happened; somehow it had gone wrong. It was an unspoken question I did not answer. She wanted to talk about what had happened when I went for help, but I was still not ready to think about all the consequences of that.

Chapter Twelve

It was that time of the year, a few weeks before Christmas, when memories of another year at that time forced their way in and that I wanted to talk to my therapist about before I would finally feel ready to open up to her about the time I had told a teacher what was happening in our home.

The sight of families shopping, shop windows displaying gifts, couples holding hands as they gazed into the festooned windows, and Santa himself, handing out toys to beaming children, had made me all too aware of how much I had lost or, if I was being honest, had pushed away. The consequences of what happened when I trusted an adult to help me were, I knew, far-reaching. For they were, I accepted when confronting my past, still affecting my adult life.

Over the days leading up to my appointment, I tried to put my thoughts in order so I could make sure that the sequence of facts was correct. I had been so unhappy then. Apart from my friendship with Sophia I felt there was nothing good in my life. What made it worse was that she, I knew, told me everything, whereas I was forced to keep a large chunk of my life hidden to others and whenever I could, to myself. But it was a secret that I felt was too big a burden for me to carry alone any longer.

It was not long after the Christmas holidays when, facing up to the New Year of 1972, heralded in a week prior, it was also the beginning of my calendar last year at junior school. Also, I was still depressed over the fact that I had seen so little of Sophia during that time. I had hoped to be invited to spend Christmas Eve with her. With money I had saved from the coins given me by my father, I had bought a present for my friend, a coat for her favourite blonde-haired Barbie doll – red, the colour of the festive season, with a tiny fake fur collar – and for her mother I had found some prettily packaged, nice-smelling soap. Both were wrapped up carefully and I had pictured them un-wrapping them after Mrs Pearson had said, with an indulgent smile, 'Well, I know it's not Christmas Day, but we can open one each on the Eve.' Maybe I would even be invited to stay the night and have Christmas morning with them, I daydreamed. After all, I believed then that I was almost part of their family.

To my disappointment, it was the day before Christmas Eve that I was invited. I felt a twinge of loneliness at not being included, which intensified the moment I saw a huge sparkling Christmas tree standing in the hall with a mound of parcels, wrapped in gold and red shiny paper, piled under it. In the hallway, Sophia told me her aunt and two cousins, who were nearly the same age as her, were arriving the following day. 'I haven't seen them since we moved here and I can't wait,' she said, making it abundantly clear to me that she was looking forward to their visit. I waited for her to say that I must come over and meet them. Instead she said, 'They live in Bristol and are going to take me back with them for a few days,' and I realised then not only was I not going to meet them, I was not going to see Sophia over the entire Christmas holidays either.

I felt a hot stab of jealousy at that thought, something I tried my best to hide, but she continued telling me all about her cousins, seemingly oblivious to my increasing silence. Meanwhile Mrs Pearson was her usual friendly self. 'I'm going to join you girls,' she said to me, placing plates of sandwiches and large slices of cake on the table. 'I need to sit down for a bit. I love Christmas but there's always more work than I planned for to do. I expect your mother says the same, especially as she has three of you in the house.'

I could not bring myself to tell her that my mother did very little and it was my gran who made sure that the day was a festive one.

Before I got in the car to be taken home, not only was I given presents, which on Christmas Day I found to be a soft wool red jumper with matching gloves, but Mrs Pearson gave me packages for the boys as well. She told me that she had chosen a toy car for Jimmy and some jigsaws for Ben – 'I think he will enjoy them, and here's a tray for him to put them together on. It means the puzzles won't have to be done on the table, so he won't get in anyone's way.'

'She must have worked out how much my mother would like Ben sitting in the kitchen putting a puzzle together,' I thought. There were hugs from Sophia as I left and then I was driven back to the grimness of home.

Chapter Thirteen

Christmas Eve in our house was not a night when we donned our good clothes and went to church for Midnight Mass. Nor was it one where the children could not sleep for excitement. None of us lay in bed dreaming of what Santa was going to bring. For we knew he had never appeared before.

The whole day, I miserably pictured what it would be like in Sophia's house. Lit red candles throwing their perfume through the house, the table gleaming with silver, a light meal for supper so they would not spoil their appetite for the mounds of food that would be served the following day. No doubt Christmas carols would be playing on the turntable but more than anything there would be laughter and conversation.

Sophia would be sitting with her cousins, a boy who was, she had told me, two years older than her and a girl, Julie, who was a few months younger. I pictured the girl cooing over the doll's house and playing with the dolls just as I had. And I was stabbed with the heavy pain of jealousy when I thought of her sleeping in 'my' bed.

Board games would come out once the meal was over. The adults would doubtless take their drinks into the 'lounge', as they called it, and leave Sophia and her cousins to amuse themselves. Later, the children would go to bed, tucked in by loving mothers, knowing that while they slept, their stockings would be filled. It would be Sophia and her cousins who would wake first, rub the sleep from their eyes and, amidst giggles, start unwrapping presents. Mrs Pearson would come into their room to tell them breakfast was ready for the whole family. Then they would get dressed and ready for church. Sophia had told me it was only when they returned that the main presents were lifted from under the tree and distributed.

I thought of my two presents I had so lovingly wrapped just two days ago. They were no doubt almost lost under all the ones I had seen under the tree and I felt another wave of misery at not being included.

There were few concessions to the Christmas spirit in our house. A dozen or so cards were on the mantelpiece. I wondered who had sent them for few visitors came to our house. Looking inside, I saw that apart from grandparents and a couple of neighbours I did not recognise any names.

'Your father's so-called happy customers,' my mother said sourly when she noticed me holding one.

Saying no more, she continued to unpack the small artificial tree that came out each year and placed it in the window of the sitting room before hanging a few gold and silver baubles on it. Instead of a family meal, it was fried eggs and chips that were placed on the table in front of us.

My mother's idea of celebrating Christmas Eve was to do what she did every year: put on loads of make-up, clip on a pair of glittering earrings, spray herself with perfume and then, taking my father's arm, walk down the road to the nearest pub.

'You can clean up the kitchen, Cassie. Get your brothers to help. And make sure you are all in bed well before we get back. Your grandparents are coming in the morning and I'm going to need help, so don't think you can stay up late. Understood?'

'Yes, Mum,' I said obediently and watched as she went upstairs to get changed.

'Ready,' she announced brightly to my father when she returned and after telling her she looked 'smashing', he opened the door and they were off.

I was pleased they were going out. The good thing about their absence was that we could all watch television. But first I wanted to get rid of the fug of cigarette smoke and the lingering aroma of stale frying fat that enveloped the whole of the downstairs. Hating its smell, I opened not just the windows but the back door as well, much to my brothers' annoyance.

'Cold,' said Jimmy, his bottom lip protruding in a toddler's pout while Ben wrapped his arms round his body and shivered.

'It's just to get this stink out,' I said and as a peace offering gave each of them a couple of toffees from the packet my father had slipped me.

'More of those when we watch television,' I told them. 'It's *The Gang Show* tonight, you know how you like it!' Words that made them rush into the sitting room to take their places in front of the TV. As soon as I had cleared the kitchen I joined my brothers and laughed along with them at the antics of grown men acting as though they were still small boys.

We shot up to our rooms well before eleven, though. It was unlikely our parents would come back early, we knew, but we did not want to risk it. Anyhow, our mother might just be crafty enough to ask the neighbours what time the sitting room lights were turned off. I for one would not have put anything past her. Once I was under the covers I willed myself to fall asleep. Even though I still felt miserable at not seeing Sophia, I was looking forward to my grandparents coming the next day. They were bringing the turkey with them and as usual there would be presents for us three children. My parents too would have to give us something: my mother, curiously, wanted to keep on the right side of her parents.

I was just beginning to doze when I heard the front door opening, my mother's voice shriller than usual, which told me she was the worse for wear and my father's deeper tones also thickened by drink. I clenched my fists: 'It's Christmas,' I told myself. 'He has to leave me alone tonight. She's still awake.'

It was not long after the sound of them returning had woken me up completely that I heard his footsteps on the stairs. I prayed he was just going to the bathroom. But no, my door creaked open and he was there.

'Pretend to be asleep,' I told myself but it was too late.

CHAPTER THIRTEEN

'I know you're awake, Cassie,' he said in that alcoholic slurry voice that made the hairs on my arms rise up. 'Think of me as Santa,' he said. 'Brought a little present for my special girl, you can open it in the morning,' and his hand caressed the top of my head. For a few seconds I believed that was the reason he had come to my room and, sitting up in bed, I smiled as I reached for the parcel.

'For the morning,' he repeated. 'Put it under your pillow and don't be opening it as soon as I leave the room.' As I did what he told me to, his arm went round my shoulders, pulled me into him and my chin was lifted, leaving me with no choice but to do what I did not want to: look into his eyes. The expression that made me shudder was there and before he spoke, with a cold, sinking feeling, I understood what the real reason for his coming into my room was.

'Your mum's fallen sound asleep on the settee,' he whispered. 'Snoring away, she is – too many drinks down the pub. Have to go downstairs in a moment and help her up them. Now, I think you have a present for your old man, don't you?' he added, trying to make his slurry voice sound jocular.

I shook my head. As none of us children were given pocket money and I only had what my father, when in a benevolent mood, slipped me, presents were hardly expected of us.

'Oh, I think you have, Cassie,' and his mouth with its stale smell of cigarettes and beer fastened on mine. Black spider hands were all over me. Down under the covers they went and with a quick wrench, my nightdress, the one my grandmother had given me with yellow fluffy ducks on the front, was hoisted up around my neck.

I heard the sound of his zip being undone, the sound that always made me go numb.

'Open your legs,' he told me more harshly than usual but still I tried to clench them shut. 'For Christ's sake, girl, do what you are told for once,' and those hard hands went under my bottom and raised me. He was inside me so fast the breath was crushed out of my chest. I lay motionless, my fingers clenched. In and out of me he went. It hurt; hurt all the way up to my stomach. It was over in a few seconds, seconds that seemed hours to me. 'Good girl, Cassie,' he said after he lifted his head from where he had buried it to muffle his satisfied groans as hot liquid spurted over my legs.

He climbed out of my bed. I heard the zip being pulled up and he threw some tissues down to me. 'You know what to do, Cassie, clean yourself up.' Then with a muttered goodnight he was gone and I listened to his steps going down the stairs.

Fat tears rolled out of my eyes. I thought of how I had thought I would have been spending that evening at Sophia's. If it wasn't for her cousins, I might even have stayed over and spent the morning with them. Then I would have slept in a pretty, freshly made-up bed, been kissed goodnight by someone who smelt of perfume and in the morning unwrapped my presents after giving them my gifts. Instead of that, my presents to them were still wrapped and lying under their tree. After church it would be the aunts and cousins who

CHAPTER THIRTEEN

would be sharing opening those brightly wrapped packages. Sophia and Julie would be sleeping soundly in the room we had shared while I was lying in my bed with my legs left sticky from my father.

Oh, how I wanted it all to stop.

Chapter Fourteen

Instead of starting my session with my therapist by explaining some of the reasons Christmas was an unhappy time for me I had another matter that I felt was more urgent to get out.

'Last night I had a nightmare,' I told her. 'I know I have told you I suffer from them, that they are all about being out of control, but this was the worst one I've ever had. I still feel shaky from it.'

'What makes this one so bad, Cassie?'

'It did not stop when I woke up.'

At this I promptly took a cigarette out of my bag. My hands were shaking so much that my therapist had to take the lighter from me. She gave it a sharp click and then leaning forward, held the flame steady for me to light it.

'Thank you,' I managed to say gratefully.

'Take it slowly, Cassie. Dreams are unpredictable. They show themselves without apparent reason,' and here she smiled. 'Sometimes a surfeit of cheese has been eaten late, and I know that other times it's a product of feeling anxiety. And I certainly understand that they can be very disturbing. Tell me, did you drink any alcohol last night or watch anything on TV that was unsettling? Perhaps a book or a newspaper article could be the trigger?'

'No, I have not lapsed, if that is what you're asking. I did not even watch the news or pick up a newspaper.'

'Well then, take a deep breath, in between puffs that is, and describe what it was you saw, so that I can visualise it. That is if you can remember it, for often we cannot recall all our dreams.'

It was hearing a certain wry humour in her voice that made me relax. She was right, I told myself, it was only a dream – I had not been visited by a dark force. Phantom hands had not touched me. It was a dream, that's all it was. But why did I not quite believe it?

'First,' I said, 'I'll try and describe to you my bedroom. I've tried to make it my peaceful place. Painted it white, chosen pink bedding and a pair of pretty bedside lamps. I dab lavender on the pillowcases in the hope that its particular scent will help chase those nightmares away. You see, I like reading there. I pile up the pillows behind me so I am propped up. And then, when I feel my eyelids drooping and I am ready to switch off the light, I toss them to the other side of the bed, all three of them. And I suppose I don't bother whereabouts they fall.

'I'm telling you that because it was them that made it worse.

'Some of the nightmare is disjointed – dreams are, aren't they? In the morning they seldom make sense. But the end of this one isn't; it is still frighteningly clear to me.

'I was in a house. Downstairs there was a child, a little boy, and he was lost. I wanted to reach him. I tried walking across the floor – a concrete one, painted blood red – but it bubbled under my feet, clinging to my shoes, making it almost impossible to move one foot in front of the other. I started to feel frightened. What would happen if it set and I was stuck there for ever?

'The little boy was crying, his arms reaching out to me. Blond, he was, and he looked a little bit like Jimmy had a long time ago.

'It was then that a dark figure appeared. Without seeing his face, I knew it was a man, and he could walk on that red, wet concrete. He grabbed hold of the child, threw him into the darkness behind him, and I could hear the child's desperate cries growing fainter and fainter until they ceased completely. And when I could hear them no longer, he strode across to where I was and lifted me up. I wanted to struggle; I tried, but no part of my body seemed able to move. It was as though my muscles were paralysed.

'It seemed the only part of me that would obey my mind's instructions were my eyes and as I moved them I saw, staring down at me triumphantly, the face of my father. His eyes were glittering, his mouth curled up in a smile, but it was not the smile of the nice father: I knew what he wanted.

'I tried to say "Put me down, put me down," for he was carrying me towards the stairs. Even in my dream I knew my bed, the one my still-sleeping self was in, was at the top of them.

'"My special girl," he was saying. His breath, the breath of the dead, stinking like chunks of rotten meat, engulfed me as he carried me into the bedroom. He placed me on the bed, *my* bed, with its pink sheets and its lavender-scented striped pillowcases, and still I could not move. I could feel him, though; feel his body sliding in beside mine, and his hands crawling over my body, touching my breasts. I tried and tried to call out; I was straining my throat with the effort, until finally a sound burst out of it: "Get off! Get off me!" it shouted in a voice so harsh I did not recognise it as mine. My eyes opened, I was awake, but he was still there beside me. I could hear his breath. I raised my arm, thumped his form only to find my clenched fist sinking into the softness of the pillows I had tossed aside earlier.'

'What did you do then?'

'I got up, put all the lights on and lit a cigarette. I was too scared to go back to sleep because sometimes when I do, I can step back into the same dream. I made myself stay awake for about an hour. I've never dreamt about him before – I know I have those dreams about not being in control, but this one was so bad. And for me, what made it even worse was that I was not a child in that dream, I was the person I am today. And it was my bedroom he was in, my special place where I had always felt so safe.'

'Cassie, your father is dead. He can never harm you again. It's the memories that have done that.'

'I know that, but I felt him in my room: his presence. It's as though he won't go away. He never wanted to let me go when he was alive and now ...'

'It was a nightmare, Cassie, introduced into your mind by your own fears. That is why it is important to continue with what we are doing. Once we have worked through more of what's been troubling you, we will work on how you can put the past firmly behind you.'

'Will I, though? Am I ever going to be able to do that?'

It was partly because of my unhappiness about Christmas, and partly because I realised this was the year that I would go to the senior school, that prompted me to seek help. If I left it any longer, I thought, it would be too late. Once I was at a new school I would not know any of my teachers; I would have no idea which one I might be able to trust. And even if I could find one I thought would listen sympathetically to my story, I knew I could never bring myself to approach a stranger. I wanted to find a grown-up who would sort everything out for me and that person had to be someone I knew and trusted.

In the end it was the teacher who taught us art and handicrafts that I chose to unburden myself to. Over the five years since I had started school, she was the only one I had allowed myself to believe I had some rapport with. She had never criticised me, or implied my clothes and hair needed washing, or made fun of my rather inept work. Instead she had praised some of my drawings and even hung a few up on the wall. Because of that, I felt she liked me. So I screwed up my courage and holding back till my classmates had left, approached her after one of the lessons. Receiving a friendly smile, I was emboldened to ask if I could come and see her when school finished.

'Of course you may, Cassie,' she replied without asking me why.

It was not until I had walked out of the classroom that the reality of what I had just done dawned on me: I was actually going to tell someone the truth about what was happening to me at home. For the rest of that day my stomach fluttered with a combination of fear of being able to find the right words to describe what my father was doing to me and relief that I was handing my problem over to an adult. I gave little thought as to what might happen afterwards. For what would happen then was, when I tried to picture it, an empty canvas.

All that day questions about the impending meeting whirled around in my head. Not only was it difficult to concentrate on my lessons, I also found it hard to make any conversation with Sophia, something I never usually had a problem with.

'What's the matter, Cassie?' she asked more than once, only to receive a muttered 'nothing'.

By the end of the day my stomach was churning so much that I felt quite faint and as if I was going to vomit. When I heard the end-of-day bell ringing to announce we were free to leave, part of me wanted to do exactly that and run straight home. I even planned what I would say to Miss Tomlin, if she even asked, what happened to me that afternoon. I would be vague and say something like I had just wanted to ask some questions about senior school.

'Don't be stupid, Cassie,' I admonished myself. 'If you tell her what's happening she'll know what to do, how to make it all stop.'

No sooner did the comforting word 'stop' come into my head than my subconscious filled my mind with even more questions. Would this really be the end of my problems? Would my favourite teacher actually step in and help me? Would she call in the Headmistress, tackle my parents? Of course she would do all of those things, I told myself. These were the thoughts racing through my mind when I made my way to her classroom, my steps faltering with apprehension. Over that short walk I started to feel lighter for hadn't I decided to jettison my burden onto my teacher's shoulders? And for that very short journey I became full of the untrustworthy emotion of hope.

'You know,' I told my therapist, when I had reached the part of my story when I entered the classroom, 'whenever I try and visualise her now, all I can see is how her warm friendly smile turned to one of cold contempt as I revealed what was happening. It certainly did not take long for me to realise that I had made a huge mistake. In fact, by the time I had barely managed to stutter out no more than three sentences and saw that look replace her smile, I realised I had read her completely wrong.'

Then, not waiting for the therapist to comment, I continued describing the rest of what happened in that meeting.

'What is it you want to see me about, Cassie?' my teacher had asked in her normal friendly way. 'Is it about your schoolwork?'

'No, Miss, it's my father,' I had blurted out. 'I'm scared of him. I don't want to stay at home any longer.'

'Oh, I'm sure it's not that bad now, Cassie. What is your problem with him? Do you think he's too strict?'

At that, I tried to find the previously unspoken words to describe what my life was really like. 'He kisses me,' was all I managed to say.

'Well, Cassie, fathers often kiss their children. That's what fathers should do. There's nothing wrong with that. So is there anything else?' she asked, her head down, giving the impression that the papers she was marking needed more attention than I did. Of course, I understood she was trying to dismiss me; that she simply did not want to hear any more. But even though her sudden coolness was beginning to drain what little courage I had left, I was determined to make her listen. I hadn't come this far in my plan not to go through with it. This was probably going to be my only chance. If I did not unburden myself to her, I knew I would never be able to pluck up the courage to try again.

'He touches me too, Miss,' I said.

'That certainly made her look up,' I said wryly to my therapist. 'I knew when her eyes met mine though all she wanted was for me to disappear. Then she could go home and push those words firmly out of her mind. No, she certainly did not want to hear any more, but nothing was going to stop me then. The bit was firmly between my teeth and somewhere inside her, a faint sense of duty made her ask, "Touches you how, exactly?"'

CHAPTER FOURTEEN

I thought back to that day and continued to recount all the details and how it had all gone horribly wrong.

I answered Miss Tomlin's question by simply saying, 'You know, Miss.'

'No, Cassie, I don't know,' she said abruptly, her voice tinged with exasperation.

'Down there,' I said, my face burning with shame as I pointed to the part of my body below the waist.

Now, in these days of awareness of child abuse, I find it hard to believe her reaction. But this happened 20 years before Childline was founded and even longer before the atrocities committed against children by some priests in the Catholic Church and those running children's homes made the headlines. But it might just as well have been during the years Queen Victoria sat on the throne, not just four decades ago.

Sexual abuse was simply not talked about. The police had no interest in domestic violence; it was as though it was accepted by a male-dominated society that women were their husband's property and as long as ambulances were not needed, whatever happened behind closed doors was purely between a husband and his wife. Not only that, it was not just accepted practice but positively encouraged for teachers to use quite brutal corporal punishment to discipline children. A child was not considered to have any rights; back then they were not seen as small people with voices that needed to be heard. So maybe now I can accept that in my teacher's life fathers did not sexually molest their children and the word 'incest' was not even in her vocabulary. However, although she did not want to accept that any abuse had happened, she was certainly capable of believing that children could fabricate outrageous stories to gain attention – although clearly not, in her experience, as filthy a story as the one I was spinning her.

'Cassie, stop this now! I really don't want to hear any more of your lies,' she told me, her cheeks stained a deep red that must have equalled the blush of shame now enveloping mine. 'I don't know how such dirty thoughts have entered your head, let alone come out of your mouth. In all my years of teaching I've never heard anything like it.' She paused a little and I could almost see cogs spinning in her head as she thought of what her next move should be. Ignoring what I had said was clearly not an option she felt she could take.

She sighed, ran her hand through her hair and looked at me almost blankly.

'Cassie, I have no other option but to take you home and talk directly to your mother. Am I the only person you have told this terrible story to?'

And that of course was the main reason she was worried.

'Yes, Miss.'

'And you have not mentioned it to any of the other children?'

'No, Miss.'

'Not even Sophia?'

'No, Miss.'

'Well, I suppose I should be grateful for small mercies at least. Now, get your school bag, we are leaving.'

CHAPTER FOURTEEN

And so the woman who could have changed my life, without consulting anyone else, made her implacable decision: she had decided in those few brief moments when I stood in front of her, my fists clenched, my face flushed, that she was not going to be the person involved in repeating a story so distasteful. She would not have to be questioned by either social workers or the police.

She must have felt some relief that this was my last term at the school. Once I was safely in the senior school she was unlikely to ever see me again. But surely that little niggling question must have popped into her head at least once: 'It couldn't possibly be true, could it?' Quelled quickly, I am sure, with the reassuring unspoken words, 'Of course it couldn't.'

I am sure that all of this was running through her mind while I stood in front of her desk, red-faced and tearful. That is the only explanation I can still find for the decision she made, an error of judgement she tried to justify by saying, 'I really ought to report this to the Headmistress, Cassie, but if I did, it would certainly cause trouble. And I am thinking of your mother. I am sure she will find what you have told me very upsetting. But it would be even more embarrassing for her if she knew I had repeated it to others, especially the Headmistress. No, I really want to spare her that.'

'Why,' I wanted to say, 'why do you want to spare her? It's me you know, me you are responsible for, not her; me who's come to you for help.' But the words stuck in my throat and refused to pass my trembling lips.

'Best if as few people as possible know about your horrible made-up stories,' Miss Tomlin continued, not giving me time to put up an argument, even if I had been capable of it. 'So,' I heard her say, 'I am going to deal with this myself. Get your school things and wait for me in the car park, I'm coming back home with you today. Better get this over as soon as possible.

'And before you ask, the answer is, no, I am not going to send you home with a note that you just might lose. Neither am I going to write a letter that might not get past the mat and into her hands. I want to make quite certain that she is aware of the appalling stories you are telling people.'

With those words she had done as I had just a few minutes prior: she had decided to jettison her burden of responsibility onto another's shoulders. She wanted my story to go away and what better person to make sure that happened than my mother?

'But Ben and Jimmy ...' I started saying.

'They can walk back without you. We'll tell them that when we go outside,' which she did while I stood mutely beside her. My two brothers, once it had sunk in that they were to leave without me, mumbled that they understood. I saw Ben's head bend so that he could hear what Jimmy was saying, watched him nod his head in agreement, and then they took off as fast as their legs could carry them. Even Ben must have been aware that a teacher visiting a parent's house could only mean one thing: trouble. No doubt Jimmy had told his brother that it might win them a few points if they got home as quickly as possible and in time to warn our mother.

I knew there was no escape from what was to happen next. The moment I had uttered the word 'touches' Miss Tomlin had decided to place me in a box of her choice and label me not as an abused victim but a lying problem child.

If I had felt nervous at the beginning of the day, it was nothing compared to how I felt by the end of it. My dread had turned into a cold hard stone lodged somewhere between my chest and my stomach. Those sparks of hope that I had fanned into believing that I might be putting an end to my father creeping into my room and forcing me to take part, in what, even the teacher considered to be, unmentionable acts, were extinguished. Nothing was going to work out as I had hoped. Whereas, up to when I had approached my teacher, I had felt I was in the right, by the time we were less than halfway to our house, I no longer did. My parents were going to be beside themselves with anger at what I had done. After all I had maligned them behind their backs and in our home that would be unforgivable. I could not even bring myself to picture my father's rage when he was told. My punishment would be severe. Tears were stinging my eyes and I knew there was no way to stop her doing what she had decided.

That fantasy I created and let myself believe, of sympathetic arms going round me, hearing someone tell me that I was safe, that I was never going to have to go back home, had turned to ash. Not that my imagination had started to take me past that point of what would happen after I was free of my parents.

I had never really thought that aspect through. I did not know then that what my father was doing to me was actually a very serious crime. That if I had been believed, both social workers and the police would have been involved and a court case would have followed; one where I would have had to stand in front of a judge, barristers, solicitors and court officials to give evidence. Those possible consequences of my actions had never entered my head. Nor had I given much thought as to where I would live once I had brought everything out into the open. My fantasy might have been about living in a new home with loving parents, but in reality, as I learnt very quickly, that was unlikely ever to have happened. Instead it would have been more probable that I would have spent the rest of my childhood in an institution. Few families were looking for a ten-year-old to take in, especially those ones who already had children; they would not have welcomed a damaged child, especially a sexually abused one. I learnt the hard way that whereas people, when they stood apart from any involvement, would state how terrible it was, say 'Poor child, such evil parents,' once they got up close, it was different. An abused child was not one they wanted mixing with their own offspring.

No, years of abject loneliness would lay in front of me, not love.

And if I had known all that, been told it in words my ten-year-old self could understand, could I have faced it?

I do not know what I would have done is the real answer. But I do know what did happen to me: I learnt in one short, hard lesson that children are blamed for their parents' actions. And that only silence can protect us.

Throughout the years that I continued to suffer his abuse, I never asked for help again.

On that walk to our house my feet felt heavier with each step I took. If my stomach fluttered with fright earlier, now it was almost convulsed with terror.

I was going to have to hear the words I had said to the teacher repeated to my mother.

'Please, Miss,' I said when we reached our run-down estate, 'can we please forget this? I'm sorry, I'll never talk about it again.' At least that is what I tried to say anyhow, but no doubt it came out in almost unintelligible hiccupping sobs.

'No, Cassie, I can hardly overlook what you told me, can I? I have a duty as your teacher to talk to your mother. I have to be assured that nothing like this will happen again. If you were capable of saying that to me, a teacher, who you do not know outside the classroom, then no doubt you are capable of telling other children those sorts of tales as well. And that would certainly make the other parents very angry. They don't send their children to school to have them hear that sort of thing. Why, they would be asking for you to be removed from school. And we don't want that, do we? I mean, what senior school would take you if you had been expelled from your junior one?'

At this I started to cry in earnest. I told her I would be punished; I pleaded with her again not to do it, I would never talk to anyone again, I promised. But it was all to no avail. When she said, 'Well, next time you think of a story to tell, you also have to think of the repercussions,' she clearly thought that I deserved to be punished most severely.

'Do you understand?'

I did.

The one thing though that she never asked me was why I had gone to her with such a story. But then I suppose she did not want to hear the answer.

My brothers must certainly have got home fast and warned our mother that I was in some sort of trouble. They would have told her that it seemed serious. I wonder if she guessed what it might have been. Had that fear of exposure lived with her ever since it had all started?

Had she, that eventful day, finally believed she was going to be tackled for letting it happen to me? If she had, then she certainly handled the situation with a smoothness that I would never have thought her capable of. But then, if she also lived with fear, then she must have planned how she would deal with the confrontations, should they ever arise.

Looking back, I think the reason for her not wanting me to have friends was her concern that I might confide in one of them. She must have been worried when Sophia came into my life. The question of whether I would confide in my new friend or her mother would surely have nagged endlessly at her. It makes sense now when I gather my thoughts as an adult; what I had seen as scathing comments and bad temper had been warnings.

'Mind your manners in that house,' she told me more than once, 'they're not the same as us.' Something I was already aware of. Then there was the specific warning that she definitely did not want me to ignore: 'And don't be talking about our business. You would not want to say anything that could stop your precious invitations now, would you?' Those were cautions that as a child, I had naively taken to mean not discussing how my father made his living or their drunken nights out down at the pub. So I never questioned what she meant, just answered, 'No,' for of course I did not want those treasured visits to come to an end.

My father, on the other hand, clearly had been arrogant enough to believe that I was never going to talk, convinced his control over me was far too strong.

That day when my mother heard that a teacher was escorting me home she would have been aware of just how unusual that was. For if it was some misdemeanour I was guilty of, then the Head Teacher would have contacted her, not the one who taught us art and needlework. If alarm bells were ringing loudly in her head, she still managed to open the door to us without any sign of being perturbed. In fact, she even managed to give a little start of surprise as though her sons had not given the news of her approaching visitor. However, I knew by the speed the door was opened and the fact it was she and not Jimmy who had done it that she had been waiting for us. Her blouse, I noticed, was a freshly ironed one she must have quickly slipped on at the same time as she thought to clip a pair of demure pearl earrings onto her ears.

The respectable matron look was what she had aimed for and succeeded in. Had I not been so sick with fear, I might have admired her aplomb.

Miss Tomlin introduced herself and apologised for turning up unexpectedly. But before she could say which subject it was she taught, my mother's polite smile widened.

'Of course, I have heard of you,' she said. 'Cassie so enjoys your art lessons.'

I was too distressed to feel surprise at that comment – I had never discussed how much I enjoyed these classes since my mother's reaction when I had brought home that very first painting.

'So what's Cassie been up to that you had to bring her back? Not unwell, is she?' she asked in a voice registering concern while placing a hand lightly on my forehead.

'Oh, it's not that. I think it's better if I come inside, Mrs Cook. I'll explain it all then.'

'Of course, how very rude of me, keeping you standing on the doorstep.' And with another smile, my mother stood aside, saying, 'I hope you don't mind the mess. Families! Well, you know,' she added as though a large part of her time was spent tidying up after us.

Judging by the unusual, almost Spartan, appearance of the sitting room, my mother must have thrown everything quickly into cupboards. Not even an overflowing ashtray was lying near the settee and her collection of magazines was in a neat pile on the debris-free coffee table.

Tea was offered and accepted; that wonderful multipurpose drink that over the years I came to know as a means to show hospitality, to calm those who are receiving bad news and as a delaying tactic. Which, in my mother's case, I am sure was the latter. No doubt she needed a short time to sum up Miss Tomlin before planning her strategy.

'So,' she said once she and the teacher were seated with steaming cups set in front of them and, I could hardly believe it, a plate of biscuits, 'you had better tell me what the problem is and we can see if we can sort it out between us.'

'Well, Mrs Cook, your daughter had asked earlier on in the day if she could talk to me after the end of lessons and I thought maybe she had some problem with one of her classes, so I said yes. Anyhow, no sooner had she come into my classroom than instead of bringing up what I expected, some small problem at school, she, without any warning, started telling me a story,' and here her hand shook slightly, while her face turned a bright red. 'I just don't know where a girl of her age got it from.'

'She does that, she has a powerful imagination, our Cassie, I can say that for her,' my mother said, casting what was meant to be an affectionate glance in my direction. 'She used it to tell you some fanciful lies, did she? Well, I suppose that's not as bad as being caught smoking or getting into a fight, is it?'

By the expression on Miss Tomlin's face I was sure she would have preferred it to have been one of those misdeeds than the one she was there to talk about.

'I'm afraid it's worse,' she said and I noticed, as she slowly repeated everything I had told her, her unbecoming blush spreading down to below her collar. 'I stopped her telling me any more. I told her that's not the sort of thing I wanted to listen to. I considered reporting it to the Head, but thought no, it would be better if I came straight to you. I was concerned that she might have talked to some of her classmates, but she assured me she hadn't.'

My mother turned slightly, fixing her gaze onto me, 'Is that right, Cassie, you only told this story to Miss Tomlin?'

'Yes,' I managed to say and I saw by a fleeting expression of relief that she believed me.

'Yes, I did believe her about that,' said Miss Tomlin, 'because if she had, that would be an entirely different matter. Then I would have had to get the Head involved. Not something that any of us would want, I am sure. I would hate to think what complaints we would get from the parents if their children came home repeating what she told me. I can just imagine the outrage.'

No doubt my mother could as well, but she managed to keep an impassive expression on her face as Miss Tomlin continued talking. 'Make-believe it might be, but a very unhealthy slice of it. I just don't understand where she could have got that idea from.'

'Nor do I,' said my mother, and I could see her mind racing to think of something. 'I mean, I am very strict about what they watch on television, not that anything like that would be shown.

'It's certainly a lot worse than I could ever have imagined,' she added, 'but I am very grateful you came to me. Especially as I know, with me not coming to the PTA meetings, you might think I am not interested in what goes on with my children's schooling.

'It's not that though, it's just,' and here my mother played the sympathy card to perfection, 'I have so much to deal with here, what with my eldest boy being the way he is. Perhaps that's the root of Cassie's problem. Maybe she doesn't understand that I have to give him more attention than her. It's not easy having a boy like that.'

A tissue appeared from up a sleeve, a quick blow of the nose, a courageous straightening of the back, and in those few seconds she turned from neglectful parent to brave defender of her young, fighting the stigma of a child with learning difficulties.

'Mind you, Cassie's very protective of him, but of course he is that age now – I forget with him being the way he is that he's not a little boy physically, for he's coming into his teens and developing . . .' her voice trailed off and she lifted eyes full of concern.

As their gazes met, I saw a flash of understanding between them.

I wanted to say something, tell them that Ben had never laid a hand on me, if that was what she was implying, but I didn't – I *couldn't*.

I heard my mother's voice saying, 'I can see that I will have to spend a little more time with Cassie. I know she feels left out sometimes. Of course I will get to the bottom of this, make sure it was just all about her wanting more attention. Although, if that's the case, this was hardly a good way to go about it, was it? And again I can't say how grateful I am to you for letting me deal with it. Now then, how about another cup of tea?' She passed the biscuits and busied herself with pouring more amber liquid into the cups.

Miss Tomlin had begun to look more at ease when my mother tried another tack. 'Mind you, just a thought, *Miss* Tomlin,' she said, placing a subtle emphasis on the word 'Miss', 'maybe she hoped you might take her home with you. I know she thinks a lot of you, said you have been very encouraging to her. And you never minded staying a little later to talk to her after school.'

I did not understand then why Miss Tomlin's blush returned, but flustered she certainly became.

Seeing this, my mother gave another smile. 'I mean, it was you she sought out to tell this to, she could have gone to anyone. Even Sophia's mother and I would have heard if she had. Of course it's not your fault. Young girls can get a bit too attached at this sort of age, can't they?'

Then, I did not understand the nuances of my mother's words. It was to be several years before I did. In just those few minutes she had implied it could have been Ben who had touched me and if so, she would deal with it, or if not, it might also have been my seeking attention from a single female teacher I had grown too fond of.

Having succeeded in disarming Miss Tomlin, she said, 'Don't worry, I'll make sure that nothing like this ever happens again.'

For the second time since we had entered the sitting room, she turned to me and I read the warning in her eyes: 'Say you are sorry to Miss Tomlin, Cassie. Sorry for upsetting her and wasting her time.'

'Sorry, Miss,' I managed to mumble.

'And you don't know why you said such a thing?'

'I don't,' I said truthfully.

The one thing my mother was certain of when she showed Miss Tomlin out, shook her hand and smilingly said goodbye was that this story was never going to be repeated. But there she was mistaken. For if the whole story was not told, there were sufficient hints of it dropped to one person to have a devastating effect on me.

Once the door shut on my teacher, I was left facing a very different mother to the one Miss Tomlin had just seen. I saw not the cold fury in her eyes I was expecting, but an unusual mixture of desperation and dominance battling for control. It was the second emotion that won. Her back straightened, her arms crossed over her chest and her face, which might have fleetingly betrayed an element of vulnerability, showed scornful anger.

'I suggest, Cassie,' she said, 'that you think twice before you tell those sorts of stories to a teacher. What did you think you were doing, trying to cause trouble for your family? Who did you think would possibly believe you? Because she didn't;

and no one else will either. "Not quite right in the head," they will say, "just like her brother, it must run in the family." And your little friend, that pale girl that's so important to you? Well, if her fancy mother heard one whisper of what you have been saying, you can kiss goodbye to ever being invited to that house again. In fact, I'm surprised that knowing where you live, that stuck-up Mrs Pearson, with her fancy car and posh voice, has made you so welcome. But then, I suppose any friend for her precious daughter is better than no friends at all.' She paused for breath then, no doubt confident that I was not going to look her in the face and say the words she did not want to hear: 'But Mum, it's all true.'

'No, you didn't think it through, did you?'

'No,' I thought miserably, 'I hadn't.' But I remained silent.

'Well, if you just wanted attention, you've got it all right. Just not the sort you were hankering for. It's just as well you are changing schools. Your Miss Tomlin will never trust you now; certainly she will never allow herself to be on her own with you. So there's no point trying that again. She won't want to talk to you, be too worried about what other stories you'll make up. Now, I hope today taught you a lesson. Did it?'

'Yes, Mum,' I whispered, more tears threatening.

Seeing I was sufficiently, if not repentant, at least submissive, a spiteful tone crept into her voice as she continued talking. 'And while you're feeling sorry for yourself, do yourself a favour and have a look in the mirror. Then ask yourself who, in their right mind, would be interested in a skinny little thing like you? I mean, you are hardly pretty, are you? That's why you don't have friends, not because of Ben or where you live. Oh sorry, I almost forgot, you *do* have one. And let's face it, she's blind! So what's that saying about you? Not much, is it?'

She looked down at me as those words, like sharp darts, pierced the last little armour of pride I had left. They left me defenceless, without even enough energy to brush aside the tears that were running down my cheeks. I wanted her to stop, to let me disappear.

'Oh for God's sake, stop with your sniffling, Cassie! I'm only telling you for your own good. Trying to help you, I am really. Now, get up to the bathroom and clean your face. We don't want your dad to see you like this now, do we? And Cassie, you needn't worry about what he will say. I'm not going to tell him about this. Break his heart, it would. Why, he thinks butter would hardly melt in your mouth,' she added in surprisingly conciliatory tones.

'But I'll be keeping an eye on you, mind. Now, I've told you that if you tell any more stories it will be said you are sick in the head. And that means you could be taken from us. Put in one of those places where mental people go. And I don't want that for you. And I'm sure you don't either, do you?'

'No,' I mumbled through my tears.

'The teacher already told you that the school wouldn't want you if you had told other children this story, didn't she?'

'Yes.'

'Well then, I'm sure you believe her. Anyhow, I've had my say. I think you have been punished enough so we won't say another word about this nonsense. All right, Cassie? I'm going to forget today and I suggest you do the same. So promise me you won't try and cause any more trouble.'

'I promise,' I said.

'That was the day I really knew, without a shadow of doubt, that my mother had believed everything I had told Miss Tomlin,' I said to my therapist. 'I might not have had my eleventh birthday, but I just knew.'

'What made you so sure?'

'She did not punish me.'

'Do you think that your mother would have told your father about you confiding in your teacher?' asked my therapist.

Now this was a question that I have never been certain of the answer to.

'I really don't know,' I answered truthfully. 'It seemed so important to him that she never caught us, and equally important to her to keep up that pretence of not knowing. But she must have said something, warned him somehow – I don't know, I wish I did. It had been a close call. She would have known what the consequences could have been, if Miss Tomlin had done what any teacher should have, reported my story to the Head. God, my mother must have thanked her lucky stars that I had chosen to confide in someone who was so easy to handle.'

'Yes,' my therapist agreed, 'she had a lucky escape – well, lucky for her and your father, but certainly not for you. If it had been reported to the Head she would have been duty-bound to notify the police and social services.'

'And handed over the responsibility to them?'

'Well, that's one way of looking at it, Cassie, but it would have been the correct action to have taken. Now, of course teachers go on courses to spot abuse and the procedures are very clear, yet tragically of course it still goes undetected in far too many cases.'

'And maybe then, if they had believed me, my life would have been different,' I said wistfully. 'And why wouldn't they have? Abuse was not talked about then, there was nothing on television about it like there is now. And incest, that was the greatest taboo. So how could I have invented such a huge terrible lie? Even if, as my mother implied, I had a crush on the teacher and wanted her attention, or that it was Ben not my father who had touched me, that would never have been believed. If poor Ben had been asked a question like that, he would just have looked completely bewildered before he stuttered, "Noooo". And I suppose sooner or later the police would have come knocking on the door?'

'The police would have been there first, Cassie. Sexual abuse is a crime. It is now, and it was then. So, social services would have reported it to them before meeting you. Your mother would not have opened the door to another pleasant woman whom she might have been able to manipulate. But, by the way you have described her to me in our sessions, she was many things but she was not a stupid woman. She would have been only too aware of just how bad it could have been. And as you say, she did not go out to work. Do you know if she had a job before she was married?'

'She worked at a hairdresser's,' I answered, 'but I don't think she was a stylist. Not by the way she used to chop our hair off, anyway!'

'So she did not have a career to fall back on, which would have meant she was not only in danger of losing her husband for a few years, but also the house's breadwinner.'

'And she would have died of shame,' I said with some degree of relish at that rather pleasing thought. 'So what would have happened to me?'

'You were only ten, so you would have been removed from your home immediately and placed in temporary care until after your father was sentenced.'

'And then what?'

'Most probably you would have returned back to your mother. If she was not charged as well, that is. Certainly she would have been questioned as to how much she knew. Nowadays the police are trained to deal with domestic violence and crimes against children much more than they were then. Today's authorities find it hard to believe that the mother does not know about the sexual abuse happening under her roof. But then, although hardly a new crime, it was one that too often was never exposed. But sadly, none of that happened, Cassie, so we will never know what the outcome might have been. Now, let's talk about that time just after your mother had received the visit from your teacher.'

'There was an atmosphere in the house, a really horrible one. Both my brothers sensed it and tried to keep out of the way as much as possible. But I was not so lucky. My mother gave me various tasks to do, which kept me around the kitchen. Within the next couple of days, my father's temper worsened, only this time there were no good moods to break it up. I'm sure she must have told him something. Not all of it maybe, she would have tried to keep up the façade. If she hadn't, then she would have felt that she was his accomplice. I don't think she wanted my father to see her as that; his respect for her would have disappeared. Nor would she have wanted to admit to herself that is what she had become. No, she wanted to be the wronged woman – I reckon it gave her more power over him.

'But even if she had done her best to put the fear of God into me, she still needed to be absolutely certain that no more similar stories came out of my mouth. I think maybe she told him that I had told a teacher that Ben had touched me in a place he shouldn't. I can just imagine her saying, "Of course I don't know if that's true," but what other explanation could there be for her saying so? She probably said something like "We had better keep an eye on them, make sure it doesn't happen again. No point even talking to that idiot about it. No, it's just best if we just try and keep them apart and don't leave them alone together."

'And then perhaps she could have added that she thought it best that nothing more was mentioned to me. Then, with no more interest being shown, hopefully I would forget all about it. Anyhow, that's what I have always believed she told him. It also explains some of his later actions. The one good thing that came out of it all was that he stopped coming to my room. But I still had to take his tea and sandwiches out to the shed.'

Each time I watched my mother filling my father's mug or removing beer from the fridge, I knew it was me she was going to send. How I hated that place, with its stink of oil and dirt. I can still recall the feel of litter and cigarette tab ends under my feet. I can't understand how anyone could have worked in such a filthy mess. There were empty beer bottles just thrown in a corner, along with blackened wads of newspaper and bits of old cloth that he used to clean his tools with. And it was my weekly job to clean it all out; another task I hated.

Every time I opened the back door to take whatever he had asked for out, I was scared he would grab hold of me again. I had not forgotten the smell of his beery breath and the sound of his wheedling voice when he pressed himself against me. But he hardly glanced up when I entered, just indicated a space where I could put down whatever I was carrying and then ignored me. Not only did he not even grunt out a 'thank you', he hardly acknowledged my presence. There were certainly no gentle strokes of my head or pocket money and sweets slipped into my hand. And for a while I did not care, I was just relieved that he kept his distance. More importantly, my mother had not forbidden me to visit Sophia. This was something I had been terrified she might do; partly as a punishment and partly to make sure that I did not have the opportunity to confide in either my friend or Mrs Pearson.

Not that she had any reason to worry. I had seen that teacher's disgust at what I had told her. It was firmly etched on my mind and there it stayed, until I was well into adulthood.

'You say his temper was worse, in what way was it?' my therapist asked.

'Looking back, I think I had caused some of it, but also so had the changes in the economy at that time. He was a mechanic who was good at keeping old bangers running. I remember him telling us how happy he had been when MOT tests had to be done every three years on any car that wasn't new.

'"Money for old rope," he said as he patched exteriors, knocked out dents, relined brakes and did whatever else it took to get an old car through its roadworthy test.'

All that changed, not overnight, but over a few years. When young couples signed up for a mortgage they were introduced to the world of hire purchase. They wanted new – new furniture and new cars. My father cursed them as he saw his work levels start to dwindle. Again, my mother nagged and talked about the highly paid jobs to be had in the car factories. And that made his temper worsen even more.

That was about the time when our meals and their quality became noticeably lacking.

'Cheap white bread with a scrape of margarine became the breakfast my brothers and I were given before we went to school. It was only our school lunches that ensured we did not go all day feeling hungry. And that was something else our mother complained about: she said it was costing too much, that it would be better for us to take lunch boxes. But that was something that my father refused to allow.'

'Why do you think that was, Cassie?'

'Pride, I'd say, simple as that. I would like to think it was concern about us getting good nutrition, but I'm pretty sure it wasn't.

'"My children are not going to look that poor," was what he always said. Anyhow, whatever his reasons, at least we had one decent meal a day. And in the school holidays my grandparents would turn up with the odd chicken or a joint. And very welcome it was too.

'You know, it wasn't very nice of me, but when I saw those children with their lunch boxes, I felt a little bit superior. When I handed my lunch money over to the teacher each week I could pretend to myself that I had it because my parents loved me more than their parents did; a pretence that stayed with me until I returned home.

'My mother was always complaining that she needed more money for groceries. My father would retort with things like "Maybe you should think of giving up smoking then, if you are saying my money does not put enough food on the table." When he shouted at her on this subject she would shut up – she would rather her children went hungry than she was left without her smokes. So she just shrugged when my father said that, but I could feel her resentment of us, especially as usual it seemed much worse towards Ben.

'She took her annoyance out in petty ways. She'd cook a meal that made our mouths water and then dish it up onto two plates.

'"Not for you," she'd say snippily when she saw us looking at a pot full of casserole. "You've had your meal, haven't you? We haven't. So if you are still hungry, then get yourself some bread and put some margarine on it. Not my fault if your school hasn't fed you enough."'

As I recounted to my therapist everything I could remember about that time, I let my mind slip back to that dismal house where all of us three children walked on eggshells. We were also aware that fewer people were coming to our door to look for a reliable second-hand car. We had seen dealers' forecourts, with their immaculate polished cars on display. They seemed, judging from my father's grumbles, to be springing up everywhere.

Not that they were the only ones he blamed for his lack of business. Instead he sat, shoulders hunched and a scowl on his face, as he spouted belligerent verbal abuse against those who lived in the new developments. Although in fact this was aimed at anyone who was what he called 'middle class'.

'Stuck-up bastards,' he called them, or rather that was one of his more polite expressions. 'Think they're better than us just because they own their houses. Up to their bloody eyes in debt though, aren't they? Couldn't save up for anything, like our sort do. They want fancy new furniture straight away. And now,' and this of course was the crux of the reason behind his temper, 'they don't want good reliable second-hand cars either. Oh no, they sign up to yet another hire purchase company and the next thing you know is they're driving home in a swanky brand new one. And what do those swanky cars come with? A fucking guarantee! And they get servicing, can you believe it – free servicing! Puts the little man out onto the scrap heap. Yep, they don't want the likes of me.'

The only thing that seemed to cheer him up was the thought of the changeover to comprehensive schools: 'Those stuck-up ones must be tearing their hair out,' said my father with a degree of glee. 'Even though we've got the bloody Tories in, they're not getting rid of the comprehensive schools, are they? Not that our kids need worry about that! None of them would have been going to a grammar school anyhow, now would they?'

If his tirade against home owners made even the back of his neck go red, that was nothing compared to what he had to say about a woman (Margaret Thatcher) being in charge of children's education. 'That bloody milk snatcher,' he yelled, followed by more remarks about politics being no place for a woman, ending with, 'she's nothing but a bloody bossy bitch, that's all she is!'

Whenever I saw his temper taking over I cringed. It was not only business that was making him so bad-tempered: I knew he was angry with me. I saw those venomous sideways glances that came in my direction and even though nothing was said, I knew it all the same.

Over the weeks that I watched his rage simmer, I wondered nervously how long it would take him to explode. Every night when I was curled up in bed, I felt sick with fear of the unknown. Something had to snap. When I finally fell asleep, vibrant, frightening nightmares visited me and in the morning when I opened my eyes, I found the bedclothes twisted around my body and my pillow damp from the tears I had shed in my sleep.

Lethargy seemed to have attacked me; it was as though each of my four limbs had grown heavier during the night. Every step I took was an effort, and at school my eyes drooped with tiredness. Miss Tomlin ignored both my pallor and my lassitude, while the other teachers snapped at me for what they saw as signs of both insolence and laziness. And all the time thoughts of my father kept creeping into my head. He would not put aside his appetite for using me for very long, I was certain. Even then, I understood that much about men's desires. I knew he blamed me, but what I had not thought of was that a man like him, who could not conceive that what he did was wrong and that it was he who was to blame, would want revenge for being thwarted; and revenge he took, not on me, but on my brother Ben.

Oh, I'm sure he did not believe that Ben had also touched me. But knowing it would hurt me more to see my poor slow sibling, who was so unable to stand up for himself, reduced to a sobbing wreck, he made him his target. And whereas my mother did not want me upset, not for any altruistic feelings but because of more repercussions, she had never shown any such concerns regarding Ben's welfare.

It happened on a Saturday morning when, as usual, my father was in his shed tinkering with car parts and I was trapped in the kitchen doing chores. We heard furious shouting, not demanding tea or sandwiches, which we were used to, but great bellows of rage that stopped any conversation and raised goose pimples on my skin. Even my mother, who was seldom the butt of his temper, looked worried.

'Have you done something to upset him, Cassie? Did you say something you shouldn't?'

'No, Mum,' I answered, for although I had taken out sandwiches earlier, he had not spoken to me, nor I to him, when I had placed them on his workbench.

'Well, you must have done something,' she hissed. 'There's no one else he's seen this morning.'

But whatever it was, I had no answer for her. I just knew there was trouble coming and furtively, inch by inch, I slid along the wall until I stood as far away from the door as possible. It was only seconds later after hearing those howls of rage that he pushed it open and slammed it so hard the bang made me jump. He stormed into the kitchen, his face almost purple with anger.

'Whatever is the matter with you?' my mother asked, but for once he just ignored her.

'Where's Jimmy and that bloody spastic?' he spat out. 'One of these little bastards has taken my spanner. Thinks it's funny, no doubt. Well, whichever one it is will be laughing on the other side of his face when I catch him.' And pushing past her he went to the foot of the stairs and yelled for his sons to come down.

'In here,' he shouted when he heard their footsteps, an unnecessary order for there was nowhere else we would be at that time of day.

'Now stand there,' he ordered, indicating the space just in front of him. 'Yes, that means you too, Cassie. Unpeel yourself from that wall,' and trembling, I went and stood beside my two ashen-faced brothers.

'One of you three has taken my spanner,' he said, his voice only moderately softer than when he had ordered them down. 'And I want to know which one of you did it. I'll count to 30. If it's not in my hands by then, someone's going to suffer. Do you think my tools are toys? Well, they're not. They are how I earn the money that puts clothes on your back and food on the table.'

He then went silent and I mentally started counting. My little brother's eyes filled; he might not have understood what was so important about a spanner, far less have any idea of where it was, but he knew all right that one, if not all of us, was going to be punished. But then, neither of us knew that it had already been decided who the culprit was going to be and just what punishment was to be meted out.

'Well, now, that's 30 seconds gone,' my father said just as I finished counting myself. 'And not one of you has been brave enough to own up, so I'm going to ask each of you in turn who has taken it. And heaven help you if you lie to me. Because I will find out,' and his eyes flicked to the stick in the corner. 'You all know what will happen to you then, don't you?'

We all did.

He chose to question Jimmy first. His finger stabbed his youngest son in the chest as he asked, 'Have you got it, you little bugger?'

Mute with fear, Jimmy shook his head by way of reply.

'You're sure? If I search your room I won't find it there? Your punishment will be worse if I do.'

'No, Dad,' Jimmy managed to whisper.

'OK, stop whining like a little baby, I believe you.'

His furious glare then landed on me.

'Well, I doubt it's Cassie here,' he said as his hand shot out to hold my chin and his fingers dug into my cheeks so hard they forced my lips to pucker. He lifted my face so that I was forced to meet his eyes and looking into their icy depths, I saw not one scrap of affection.

'I mean,' he added, 'what would you want a spanner for, eh? We all know you're only interested in your fuckin' dolls, don't we? Oh, I forgot, and that stupid drawing you do instead of helping your mother more.'

'You know,' I said to my therapist when I got to that part of the story, 'it was stupid, I know, but I wanted the nice father back then. I wanted to feel I was special again. How stupid was that? I mean, he was showing me his true colours and that was what entered my head.'

'That's very understandable, Cassie. You were still a child, and however warped and inappropriate his affection was, you felt someone cared. And feeling loved is very important to children.'

At her words, I felt a stab, not just of pain but of guilt as well. Seeing that, she simply said, 'Cassie, now is not the time to judge yourself,' and sitting back, waited for me to pick up the story again.

'I remember,' I continued, 'that I was too choked up to speak. He had been so scornful when he spoke that I just looked at him miserably, while my mother stood there and said nothing about how he was treating her children.'

I closed my eyes briefly, and forced myself to bring back up the picture of us three children standing in the kitchen, terrified of the man towering above us. He was glaring at all of us before he stretched out and lifted his stick, waving it in the air before he pointed it at Ben.

'Well, there's only one other person left, isn't there? So it's got to be you, you fuckin' spastic!'

Ben tried to speak, to say he did not know what our father meant; that he had not taken anything. But as usual, when he was frightened the words stuck in his throat and turned into whimpers. Out of all of us, he was the one who had felt that stick the most. Knowing just how much pain it could inflict, he immediately flung his arms up to cover his head.

'Noooo!' he cried. Drool hung from his mouth and his whole body shook with fear.

My father gave him a disgusted look.

'Bleating like a little girly, are you? God, what did I ever do wrong to be saddled with such a pathetic piece of shit as you? Oh, shut your noise, I'm not going to hit you. Here, see, I've put the stick down, so stop this nonsense now and look at me.'

There was such a look of gratitude on Ben's face when he saw the stick laid down that I felt sick for him. I wanted to turn away, not see what was going to happen next. For I did not think for one moment our father had finished tormenting Ben. This was just a few seconds' reprieve and then it was going to get worse. I did not want to witness my brother's humiliation. Too often I had seen those livid marks that our father's stick had inflicted, curving around his legs. So just what was it that he was planning to do, if it was not to be a beating?

Of course I knew my father well and was all too familiar with his expressions and I suddenly understood by his malevolent smile that he planned something much worse for Ben than just giving him the usual bruises that time would fade. I can picture that scene so vividly, even now. I can see Ben's gangling frame, his raised arms, showing bony wrists sticking out of a jumper he had outgrown some years before, with tears and snot sliding down his face. It was the memory of his eyes though that still makes a lump rise in my throat; they were no longer bewildered but almost glazed over with fear. Ben had no understanding of what he was being accused of. He certainly had no comprehension that, innocent or not, it was being the way he was that drove my father to punish him.

'Now, look at me, Ben,' said my father and maybe it was the unusual use of his name that made Ben look at him even more fearfully. 'Oh, stop being so pathetic, standing there quaking! I told you I'm not going to raise the stick to you, didn't I?'

But Ben still remained silent, which only managed to infuriate him more.

'You've been given a lot of toys, haven't you?' he said in a whisper which carried more menace than any of his usual bellows of rage.

'Yes,' Ben answered, although in fact he had been given very little. Just a few Corgi cars, from our grandparents, that he treasured and the jigsaw Sophia's mother had given him.

'And are you grateful?'

'Yes,' the boy answered, his eyes downcast.

My father's voice, with the threat of a wheezy cough ever present in his speech, raised another octave, 'I don't think you are. Otherwise they wouldn't be all over your bedroom floor, would they? How many times have you got to be told to put them away when you're finished with them? But again you have disobeyed me, haven't you?'

Not that he had been anywhere near Ben's room that day, he just knew the few toys Ben had were the only things he had to occupy himself with.

Ben tried for the second time that morning to stutter out a few words. But again they came out as an almost unintelligible gabble.

Irritably my father turned to me: 'Cassie, I can never make out what this moron says, mumbling away as he does. You seem to understand him all right, so tell me, what's he saying now?'

'It's only the ones he was playing with when you called him down,' I answered reluctantly.

Then unfortunately for him, Ben stuttered another sentence.

'Now what did that mean?' asked my father, getting angrier again.

'He says he always puts them away when he goes to school or when he comes downstairs.'

'You're saying it's my fault, are you?' said my father, and realising he had made a mistake, an even more terrified expression settled on Ben's face. 'Are you arguing with me now, Ben? Getting your sister to argue for you?'

'No ...' he started. But he never had a chance to finish the sentence; instead a large hand slapped him so hard across the face that it sent him reeling to the floor.

'Said I wouldn't use the stick,' said my father, 'but I never promised I wouldn't hit you, did I?'

At this I looked pleadingly at our mother: 'Stop him,' I longed to say, but catching my eye, she just shrugged and continued puffing on her cigarette.

'So, not only do you take my spanner, but you cheek me as well. A beating's too lenient a punishment for you. Now go upstairs and bring me down those toys.'

Wiping his eyes with the back of his hand, Ben piched himself up and shuffled out of the kitchen. I could hear his slow steps mounting the stairs and then a few seconds later there was the sound of him coming down.

'Oh please don't take them from him,' I prayed to myself, 'they are all he's got.'

'Now, bring them over here,' my father ordered as soon as Ben came back into the kitchen, 'and put them down on the table.'

'Can you go any slower?' he asked in a derisory tone as Ben's steps faltered. And my brother, his whole body shaking with tremors of fear, did as he was told.

'Now, as you are so fond of my tools, go outside to the shed and bring me a hammer.'

Ben looked at my father, as I did, with approaching horror as a glimmer of understanding at just how cruel his punishment was going to be sunk in. But he still went out to the shed and returned with the hammer, silently handing it to our father.

I crept over to Jimmy and put my arm protectively around him, not sure whether it was to comfort him or me. I think we were both equally petrified of the malignant atmosphere pervading the room. It was making me ache inside. I just wanted my father to stop, to smile or laugh out loud and say it was all a joke; that just making Ben believe he was going to lose his precious toy cars was punishment enough. But I already knew what was really going to happen.

181

One by one Ben was made to place his little cars on the floor and raising the hammer high above his head, my father swung it down. After the first one was crushed, I shut my eyes, but I could still hear the sound of the metal and plastic splintering and the mewling noise Ben made with each act of destruction.

When I opened them again, it was to see my father red-faced with exertion and the wretched form of my poor older brother. Tears were coursing down his cheeks as he looked down to where small lumps of red, yellow and blue metal lay at his feet. I felt myself shake in sympathy at his anguish.

That was the day my little brother learnt to understand fear and my older one was forever changed. The seeds of hate and resentment had been planted. Over the next few years we would all watch them grow.

'What happened to Ben in the end?' my therapist asked when I sat back in my chair, exhausted by these recollections and the emotions they stirred up.

'You mean you don't know?' I answered, for I had assumed that after all my visits to her, there was not much she hadn't learnt about my family.

Chapter Fifteen

I tried to put that terrible day when I had sought help from Miss Tomlin behind me. I was still in one of her classes but I never attempted to speak to her again. She in turn did her best to avoid eye contact and on the odd occasion when we passed each other in the corridors, she managed to look at a spot just above my head.

The memory of her reaction was still clear in my head and I was certain she had not forgotten what I told her. She had, however, put it in a compartment labelled 'not to be believed'. I wonder now, with so many stories on the news and in the newspapers, where men, once public idols, have been charged with heinous offences against children, if she ever feels a wave of unease. Does the memory of the day she dismissed my story travel from her subconscious brain into her conscious one and start to raise doubts?

I hope so.

Not being able to see into the future where I would learn that I was not the only child whose father crept into her bedroom, I just said to myself, 'Don't think about it, Cassie. Soon you won't have to see her again.' A little sentence I used to comfort myself each time I had to go into her class.

I started counting the days until the end of term. Only a few more weeks turned into just 20 days and then ten until finally we were in the last week. Then it was my last lesson with Miss Tomlin and all through her class I kept saying to myself, 'This is the last time I will see her.' In fact, it was my dislike of having to be in her class that had given me the one reason why I was looking forward to changing schools.

Those last few days in the run-up to the end of term I was thinking of the fun Sophia and I would have over the holidays. There had been no mention of her visiting her cousins or them visiting her and the thought of visiting her family even more than I did during term time made me so happy, especially having her to myself.

It was just two days before we broke up. As I was coming out of school, I saw Miss Tomlin talking to Mrs Pearson. I remember the sky was clear and blue and no clouds marred its perfection. Behind her dark lenses Sophia's eyes were turned up to me as we chattered about the plans we had made for the first week of the holidays. Her face, I noticed, glistened slightly. I had waited for her as she went to the cloakroom and smeared on some sun cream before she ventured going through the doors. She was just telling me that her mother would take both of us swimming and I was saying I had not learnt how to, when the axis of my world froze. And just for a moment my legs refused to move.

I knew instinctively as soon as I saw them standing together. Miss Tomlin was doing the talking and Mrs Pearson listening unsmilingly. I knew that I was the subject of their conversation. Sophia was oblivious to the fact that I had stopped walking and waved to her mother and quickened her steps to go and greet her.

I had already caught their combined gaze flickering in my direction before Miss Tomlin walked away, her back rod-straight; it was a walk I recognised. It was one that simply exuded self-righteousness.

My feet felt rooted to the spot. Was I going to see the same expression of disgust on Mrs Pearson's face as I had seen on the teacher's?

'Only one way to find out, Cassie,' I told myself and then with my heart hammering in my chest, I followed Sophia to where her mother stood waiting for her.

I was no wiser that day as to what had transpired. Whatever Miss Tomlin had said, Mrs Pearson greeted me in her usual friendly way.

'I'll be seeing you on Friday,' she said before she walked away with Sophia. I tried to tell myself I had been imagining that Miss Tomlin had said anything. 'Surely,' I kept telling myself, 'if she had told her my "lies", I would not be visiting on Friday?' But once suspicion is lodged, especially suspicion mixed with fear, it does not leave the mind easily. My senses were on full alert to see if there were any differences in how I was treated when I visited.

My therapist leant forward then.

'And did she change towards you?'

'It was hard to see any difference really, but somehow I felt things had changed. She was still friendly, but there were definitely small differences in her behaviour.'

'For example?'

'Well, that Friday I had not been invited to stay over.'

'No, but you did tell me, Cassie, that it was not every Friday you stayed. That it was mainly when Sophia's father was away on business.'

'It was not just that. As you say, it was not unusual for Mrs Pearson to drive me home. No, it was the fact that she felt the need to explain the reason she had not invited me to stay. She told me that she was taking Sophia shopping; that they were going to spend the morning together for Sophia needed summer clothes as she appeared to have grown out of the ones she had. And no sooner had she told me than she blushed. Maybe she realised that talking about a whole morning spent taking her daughter shopping was tactless. And of course it was, which again was unusual for her.'

'Apart from that, was there anything?'

'Yes, I gradually became aware that Mrs Pearson seemed reluctant to leave Sophia and me alone. It was not something I noticed straight away because she often liked to chat to us in the kitchen but this time she seemed to think of ways of stopping us going up to Sophia's room. That Friday, after I had seen her with Miss Tomlin, of course I was hypersensitive to any small changes, but I was not imagining that there were some.

'When we moved to go upstairs she looked up from her baking. "Oh, don't go and hide in Sophia's room, girls," I heard her say in a voice that was almost artificially bright. Then before Sophia could argue, she added she did not get to spend enough time with us. This hardly seemed true because she was spending nearly all of the following day shopping with her daughter. Next, she suggested we all played Monopoly, and she seldom tried to include herself in those games.

'I did not think about it too much that evening – after all, the term had come to an end. No more Miss Tomlin and wasn't Mrs Pearson still being friendly to me? So in a way I was feeling as though a weight had slipped off my shoulders. Plus, she confirmed that she would be taking us both swimming. So it was not as though I was being excluded or anything like that. I remember Sophia telling me how much she loved the swimming baths as soon as her mother confirmed that we were going.

'"It's the one sport I can manage," she said gleefully, her face pink with pleasure. "All I have to do is swim in a straight line, nothing hard about that." And when I told Mrs Pearson I could not swim she laughed and said I could use a rubber ring for a while. And not to worry about it, I would soon learn.

'I suppose as a child I would not have understood what Mrs Pearson's worries might have been. Perhaps she thought that I might tell Sophia things that she was too young to hear. But as I said, she was a kind woman, so she did not want to stop me coming to the house. Not during those holidays anyhow. I am as certain now as I was then that Miss Tomlin told her something. But I never found out what it was.'

'Was there anything else that happened then?'

'There was one afternoon that I felt was a little strange. Mrs Pearson asked Sophia to fetch her something from upstairs – I think it was a cardigan. And the moment her daughter was out of earshot, she turned to me. "Cassie," she had asked, "how are things at your house? I know your mother must have her hands full."

'"Yes, she has," was the only answer I could think of.

'"And you, is everything all right with you?" and she gave me a searching look.

'"What do you mean?" I asked, stalling for time and she faltered in her response. Mindful of the warning I had received about confiding in adults, I remained silent – I did not want to see the warmth on Mrs Pearson's face wiped out too.

'Was that another lost opportunity? Would my life have been different had I told her? I don't know.

'What I do know is that she never invited my brothers to join us during that summer.'

Chapter Sixteen

A week after I had told my therapist about the nightmare that had disturbed me so much, I arrived for my appointment looking tired and strained. The dark circles under my eyes surely announced on their own another night of restless sleep.

'I had the same dream again,' I blurted out before I had even taken a seat.

'And?'

'I remembered what you told me, that it was only a dream and that's all it was.'

'And how did you feel, Cassie, when you accepted that however unpleasant your nightmare was, it could not harm you unless you let it?'

'I felt sick, if I'm being truthful. I didn't want to go back to sleep. I was frightened that if I did, I would be sucked straight back into that darkness.'

'So what did you do?'

'I made myself get up and make a cup of tea. And I told myself over and over it was only a dream. Oh, and I forgot about my "no smoking in my bedroom" rule and lit one.'

My therapist smiled then.

'Here's what I tell my patients, Cassie. Therapy is not a magic cure. It does not stop nightmares or being afraid of the dark, which you have told me you are.'

'So what does it do then?'

'It helps you to deal with your fears, which is not the same as making them disappear. When you told me you were afraid of the dark, what did I tell you to do?'

'Leave a light on and I took your advice on that.'

'But more than that, Cassie, you have rationalised that your dreams cannot harm you, which is good. It means you are beginning to take control.

'I think you have come to understand that nightmares are a sign of anxiety. And of course in your case it is made worse by having bad memories that have still not been dealt with. And that is what we are working towards. During your waking hours you manage to suppress a lot of those negative thoughts about your past, but of course you are far more powerless when asleep.

'You did the right thing though, made yourself wake up fully and then dismiss what you had seen, while being in that half-awake state, as being part of a bad dream. Now, at our next session, I want to cover more about what happened between you and Sophia that affected your friendship.'

'Why do you wish to talk about that especially? Surely we have more important subjects to cover than a friendship from my childhood?'

My therapist took no notice of the sullenness I was beginning to show. Instead she said very calmly, 'Do you remember our first meeting, Cassie? And what I told you then?

'That it is the root of our problems that we have to examine. And to do that we have to go back to when they began,' I said wearily.

'Good, Cassie, and that is what we are doing here. And then between us we have to look at how you dealt with the problems that affected your life then and how you might deal with them now.'

'You mean you think I might not have handled them right?' I asked, feeling defensive.

'No, you were a child and children only see what is in front of them. But the adult you are now might begin to see things a little differently. So make some notes and we will talk about that next week.'

That was the session that made me want to throw in the towel. 'Where exactly are we going with it?' I asked myself. Talking about my younger self and looking to see what mistakes I might have made was not something I wanted to do any longer; I was beginning to resent bringing everything I had tried to put behind me out into the open.

'What good is it doing?' I asked myself. 'It's too late to help the child I was once.'

I wanted to scream at my therapist, to make her see my desperation and understand that it was me – me the adult – who needed help. Why couldn't she see that? Those and other thoughts like them churned angrily in my head until

I alighted from the bus and walked the short distance to my house. 'My empty house,' I said to myself miserably. 'Just how far have I progressed?' I asked myself again, as I fell despondently onto the settee.

'Stop feeling sorry for yourself, Cassie,' my sensible inner voice told me sternly. 'You *have* progressed. You can't blame your childhood forever, you've made plenty of mistakes all on your own. And,' the voice continued, 'you have watched enough television and read enough newspapers to know that yours is not the worst story in the world, even though you might like to think it is. So no, you are not going to the off-licence, you are going to make tea and get your notebook out.'

I listened to that voice, not that I had much choice in the matter, and after a while I reluctantly obeyed it. I made the tea, then picked up my notebook and scribbled down notes as I forced my mind back to the events that took place in the summer of 1973.

It took me several days to remember everything and put it in order and then write it down again. To begin with I had to force myself to bring up those memories but to my surprise, I was able to smile at some of the nice ones that also began to emerge. Over that week I came to realise not all of them were bad. Even more importantly, I found that instead of feeling resentful at the task my therapist had set, I was finding comfort in thinking back to the time I had spent with my grandmother. Before I knew it, my notebook was full of my scribbles, and it was time for my next appointment.

Chapter Seventeen

The part of my story that my therapist wanted me to talk about had started, not when I learnt that I was to start senior school alone, but when my grandmother informed me that she was taking me shopping.

'Now that must be a good memory,' was the only comment my therapist made when I recounted the story I had written down.

'Yes, it was,' I agreed, and giving her a wry smile, I continued. 'You were right, I had forgotten there were some and I know I have been dwelling only on the bad ones.'

I could tell by the respondent expression on her face that she was pleased by my acknowledgement of this.

'You know, Cassie, good memories are very important. When they come into your head you must cherish them. They are something we can take out, look at and feel the warmth of them, no matter how many years have passed. And I think you are beginning to understand that. Now, tell me about the time your grandmother took you shopping.'

Glancing at my notebook occasionally, I let my mind drift back in time and for 30 minutes I described what had happened.

It was not long after the start of the school holidays that my fear of going to school in shabby hand-me-downs was removed. But up until then I was as usual not paying much attention to what was happening around me. If I had, I might have come to learn sooner that my life was about to change, and not for the better. Certainly I would at least have asked questions of Sophia. And whereas there were things she did not want to tell me, doubtless her mother had encouraged her to keep quiet, she was not a child capable of telling untruths.

I was haunted by the image of all the other girls in new uniforms and me standing out as usual because of what I had to wear. But then my grandmother informed me that we were to spend a day together selecting everything I would need when I started my new school. I was too excited at the thought that I was going to have a wardrobe of new clothes to notice anything amiss. Not only was she going to buy my uniform but I was to have jumpers and skirts to wear out of school hours as well.

Throughout my last junior school term I had dropped hints to my mother that the uniform at the senior school was a very different one. These remarks, much to my consternation, had very little impact on her. Over those weeks I became certain that she was just going to send me to the next school wearing my old school uniform.

'It's not worn out yet, is it?' she had told me with a mocking glint in her eyes.

At that remark, and others like it, I could almost hear the titters of amusement my appearance would cause. As my father still had not shown signs of forgiving me for the teacher's visit, I knew I could not expect any support from him either.

Although I had not confided in my grandmother, she must have picked up that I was worried about starting my new school.

'Has your mother taken you shopping yet?' she asked me one afternoon when I was visiting her. I sensed somehow it was a question she knew the answer to and my woeful reply of 'No' just confirmed it.

'Mmm,' was her only comment but when I made a move to return home, to my surprise she announced that she was coming with me.

'Just want a little chat with my daughter,' was all she said although her tone implied this was not going to be idle chatter.

I still don't know what was discussed that day, but clearly my grandmother had put her foot down. Luckily for me she was the one person who, apart from my father, my mother never wanted to upset. It was my mother who called me into the sitting room.

'Your gran has something to tell you,' she announced before adding that she had to start getting supper ready and would be in the kitchen if we wanted her.

As soon as she had gone my grandmother told me that she was the one who was going to sort out my new uniform.

'Your mother has given me the list that has been sent out by the school,' she said, brandishing the printed list, which was crumpled and tea-stained. 'And next week I am taking you shopping.'

At the thought that I was not going to have to attend senior school in my old school clothes those lead weights of worry lifted from my shoulders and evaporated into thin air. I stifled a gasp as my eyes brimmed over with tears of relief and gratitude.

'Oh, thank you, Gran,' I managed to say before throwing my arms around her.

'Now then, Cassie love, no need for tears,' she said gruffly, patting my back. 'What I want you to do is help me make a list of everything else you will need. Don't want to forget anything, do we? I know it's a grey skirt and jumper plus a green blazer as well as an overcoat. Now, apart from a couple of white shirts and the school scarf, what else do you think you will need?'

I was silent for a moment as I heard the echo of my mother's voice ringing in my ears from the previous year when my grandmother had taken me shopping for new boots.

'Don't you be asking for everything you see, mind. Your gran's not made of money. She only has state pension to get her through the week and God knows, that's not very much,' she had told me just before Gran arrived to collect me.

Seeing my hesitation, my gran chuckled. 'Come on, Cassie, I can see by the look on your face there's something. And if you're worried about the cost, don't be. I've got a little put away and what better use for it than to spend it on my only granddaughter, eh?'

'Gym clothes, Gran,' I blurted out, still uneasy at saying it, for heeding my mother's warning, I did not want to appear greedy. I knew, because my mother had told me more than once, that they were not cheap. But there was no denying I longed to have them. It was one thing to do gym in your knickers as a little girl, another thing altogether at senior school.

'Of course you will need those,' Gran said without any hesitation, 'and while we're at it, some new knickers and vests as well. Looks like you've done a bit of growing recently, so I'm sure the ones you have are too small.' I noticed her give a barely concealed disapproving glance at my too-short skirt and the hand-me-down jumper of Ben's, which was worn thin, both at the cuffs and elbows.

'Oh, and I'd better put down school shoes on my list as well,' she added, 'and don't worry, I know you will have to have gym ones as well. I want you to look smart on your first day, Cassie. I was your age once, so I know it's important.

'We'll spend the day in town. And once we've finished with shopping, we'll treat ourselves to tea at Lyons, what do you say?'

Too choked up to say much, I felt my face stretching into the widest smile it was capable of.

It was the following Monday that Gran arranged to collect me – 'Not so busy in town then,' she gave as her reason. Although it was a day I had been invited to go swimming, the pride I felt later at being able to say to Sophia, 'Sorry I can't come, my gran's taking me shopping for new school clothes,' outdid the disappointment I would usually have felt.

'I expect you got yours when your mother took you shopping?' I added and assuming the answer was 'Yes', I hardly paused in giving her all the details of the planned shopping spree and the Lyons tea I was being taken to.

I should have noticed then that she had not answered me. Nor, had I thought about it, apart from a swimsuit, had she shown me any of the new clothes her mother had bought for her. Maybe I thought then she was being tactful, but I can't remember now why I was not more curious.

What I do remember though is the whirl of shops my grandmother and I visited. How, after various items of uniform had been packaged up, I was sent to a changing room to try on casual skirts and pretty coloured jumpers. Then there was a shoe shop, where my feet were measured and my grandmother let me choose the new Clarks slip-ons, and finally, eating a huge pink and white meringue with cream in the middle at Lyons. It was when I was tucking into it that I felt Gran watching me. Her sharp blue eyes filled with concern were staring down at me and our gaze met.

'Cassie,' she had said, 'if you ever need to talk, you know you only have to come to me, don't you?'

'Yes,' I mumbled, for part of the un-swallowed meringue was still lodged in my mouth as I savoured its gooey sweetness.

CHAPTER SEVENTEEN

*

At this I looked up at my therapist and thought for several seconds.

'The question I have never really answered is why didn't I talk then? After all, I was close to her and she must have felt there was reason for concern.'

'I thought you were going to ask me that. You have asked yourself, so what was the answer you came up with?'

'First, I told myself it was because I did not want to cause her and Grandpa any distress. I mean they were old, weren't they? Or at the age I was then, they seemed very old to me. But now, I think it was really because I thought either I would not be believed or even worse that I was, and that my grandparents would blame me. And then they wouldn't have loved me any more. So maybe that was another opportunity that I allowed to slip away.

'She took me back to my home after that. I can still hear the sniff of disapproval from my mother when she saw us loaded down with so many bags. But she did not say anything, just thanked her mother and told me to put everything away.

'You know, it was just so wonderful being in my room surrounded for the first time in my life by a pile of shopping bags. Gran had thought of everything, even bought me some coat hangers so I could hang them all up. And as I unpacked each garment, I held them up to my nose just to sniff their smell of newness.

'When my blazer and coat were hanging up on the back of my door and I had folded up everything else neatly, I felt a twinge of something approaching excitement at the thought of putting them on and going to my new school for the first time. You know, just the realisation that I was not going to be that scruffy girl with grey underwear, but a smartly dressed one, had taken away my fears. And not only that: this time I would not be walking through the gates with my brothers, but with my best friend.

'That is what I believed then, and for the next few weeks I was happy.'

My therapist had scarcely interrupted me when I told her of that time but I knew from the expression on her face that she had been listening intently.

'So what happened afterwards, between then and your first day at school?' she wanted to know.

'Everything changed.'

Chapter Eighteen

'It was near the end of those holidays when I learnt that I was to be starting my new school on my own. And despite her reassurances I knew, even if she didn't, that I had lost Sophia. Somehow, even though Mrs Pearson had been her usual friendly self during those summer days, I had often felt a change was coming. That knot of anxiety had taken root the moment I saw Miss Tomlin talking to Sophia's mother. In her own way, my mother tried to warn me.'

'How did she do that, Cassie?' asked my therapist.

'It was when I was brought back on a Friday night, which marked three weeks of not being invited to stay over. I must have looked despondent. My dad was out and my mother was, as normal, watching television. But for once she took time to look up. "Nice day?" she asked and taken aback at her show of interest, I just mumbled, "Yes, all right." She asked me to make her a cup of tea.

'"Cassie," she said, once I had handed it to her, "don't get too dependent on Sophia. You have to understand that although her parents might like the fact their daughter is happier now she has a friend here, that doesn't mean you figure in their plans for her future."

'"What do you mean?" I had asked.

'"Just that people like them have different ambitions for their children than people like us. Mind you, put one step wrong and you won't figure in the present either."

'She turned back to the television, which marked an end to our brief conversation. I left the room feeling angry. Yet again she was trying to spoil something that made me happy.'

'And now? How do you feel about it now?'

'I think she knew something. Like I said, Mrs Pearson was a kind woman. I think it's possible she spoke to my mother. I mean, my parents were quite lenient that summer. They never once stopped me going to visit Sophia. My mother even came to the door sometimes when Mrs Pearson dropped me off. And the other thought that has come to my mind is that she was worried that Miss Tomlin might just have said something so her opening the door to me was her wanting to present herself as a caring mother. Anyhow, it's too late to find out her reasons now.'

'So how did you find out that Sophia was not going to the senior school with you?'

'She finally told me. Her mother must have said it was not fair for me to be thinking we were still going to start the new term together, especially as so much of my conversation was about plans I was making that included both of us. We were in the kitchen and Mrs Pearson had for once left us alone.'

As I started to tell my therapist about it, a picture of that afternoon slid into my head. The memory was still clear and sharp as though it had been only a few days earlier that I listened to Sophia, her cheeks the reddest I had seen them, informing me about something she had known right from the start of the holidays.

I was voicing my fears about facing another school where the work would be more difficult rather than showing any real enthusiasm for the new challenge. At least we were facing it together, I added, but it was still a shame that we could not sit next to each other.

'But there will be the breaks and lunchtimes,' I had said uneasily, aware that the only response I was getting was silence.

'Cassie,' she had said, and just the way my name came out of her mouth sent a warning that I was about to hear something I would not like. So, ignoring her attempt at interrupting me, I did not pause in my babbling about any good point I could think of.

'Wouldn't it be great if they had a swimming club with races? I mean, you are so good, that's something you would easily win. Why, they might even ask you to swim for the school,' I enthused, while my brain raced ahead, searching for more positive remarks to make. Was I using words as a barrier to protect myself from hearing something I did not want to? I'm sure I was. I must have believed that if I spoke for long enough, the words I did not want to hear would vanish into thin air.

'Cassie,' she said again, this time a certain firmness in her voice, 'please listen to me,' and I stopped mid-sentence and waited.

'I'm not going to the same school as you.'

'So what school are you going to then?' I asked, still not wanting to accept what I knew was coming for I did remember her telling me how one day she was going to a school where everyone was like her. Even though she had told me this would not happen for a long time, it was something that had lingered in the back of my mind.

'That is what she is going to tell me,' I thought, and sat very still as I waited for what I knew was to come.

'It's not near here,' she said.

And by that short sentence she confirmed what I had already suspected.

'It's the school you told me about, isn't it? The special school?'

'Yes, it's for children like me. Some of the pupils were born blind while others, like me, can see, but all of us will have bad eyes. I won't be different there,' she said and I caught the sadness in her voice then.

'But you told me that we would be going together. That you would not go to that other school until you were older,' I persisted.

'I know – I was telling the truth, Cassie. But my parents have changed their minds.'

'So what made them change?'

'My father said,' and here she paused and her brow furrowed as she tried to repeat his exact words, 'that delaying would be more disruptive to my education.'

Her cheeks grew even pinker as she carried on talking.

'Cassie, my parents decided that now I have to leave junior school it would be better if I only had one change. If I went to the local school with you I could not finish my education there. They would not be able to cater for all my needs when I got older.

'My eyesight is getting worse. I will never be able to do the things the other girls can. I can't even jump over a skipping rope and I'm not ever going to be able to ride a bike, far less drive a car when I am grown up. And soon the writing on the blackboard will become more blurred. It will be harder doing my homework. I'll never be able to keep up with the others.'

I wanted to say something nice; to tell her I was sorry about her eyes and that I understood. But those treacherous tendrils of resentment were twisting around my inner self. So instead of being understanding of her situation, I lost my temper.

'You've known all this time,' I yelled. 'You've lied to me. Best friends are supposed to tell each other everything.'

Sophia gave me a startled look. I doubt anyone had ever spoken to her like that before. As soon as my angry words left my mouth, I regretted them and even more so when I saw her eyes fill with tears.

At this stage I sat back in my chair and felt the prickling behind my own eyes as they looked at the therapist.

'I should have said sorry, of course I should. I knew that then and I know it now, but instead I just sat frozen with hurt and a feeling of betrayal.'

205

'What happened afterwards?'

'Sophia ran from the room and Mrs Pearson, giving me an angry look which silently said, "Stay where you are, Cassie," followed her. She was only out of the room for a few minutes but it was long enough for me to feel both embarrassed and remorseful. When Mrs Pearson came back into the kitchen, she just told me she would drive me home. I thought she would be angry with me, but instead she told me she understood, but that it would be for the best if I left coming back to the house for a few days.

'"I want Sophia to calm down. This is not an easy time for any of us – including you, I know, Cassie. You'll miss her, I know, and so will I. And it is not easy for Sophia herself to move away from home for several weeks at a time," and her voice was gentle as she said, "I'm sorry for telling her not to let you know sooner. That was my fault, not hers. I just did not want to spoil the last few weeks I'm going to spend with my daughter for a while and I did want both of you to enjoy the time as well."

'She told me to come over on the Friday afternoon – "And stay for tea, I'll drive you home afterwards," and once again I noticed that she had made it clear that I would not be staying for the night.'

As though reading my thoughts, she continued to say, still in that gentle voice, that the whole family had to get up early on the Saturday morning as they were taking Sophia to where her boarding school was: they wanted to get her settled in over the weekend.

That was when I became convinced that Sophia was leaving not because she needed to be with children who had similar problems to hers, but because of Miss Tomlin. Whatever she had said to Mrs Pearson had worked: I was being separated from my only friend. This belief became lodged in my head and stayed there for most of my life.

All this happened three days before I was to start at the senior school.

'And what happened on the Friday when you visited?' my therapist asked.

'Before I could apologise to Sophia, she got in first. Said she knew she should have told me before. She looked so upset when she told me that, and even more so when she said she was going to miss me as well, that I felt worse with every word she uttered.'

I was still feeling tearful at the thought of her going, but I managed to say I was sorry I had shouted. And then we ran out of words. All I could do was look at her – I just could not find anything nice to say. For the first time since I had met Sophia, I wanted the visit to end. You see, I understood that whatever she was telling me, underneath she was looking forward to going. I'm not saying that she was not apprehensive about leaving her home, but we all want to belong, don't we, be accepted and not be seen as different? And at the special school she would, as she had told me, be the same as the other children. And that alone would have made her look forward to going. Young as I was, I was still old enough to understand that and also know that once there, she would make new friends, which would of course change our relationship. Maybe if I had been older, just a little more mature, I would have said all that; reassured her that I was pleased for her and wanted her to be happy. But at 11, I just felt miserable. Tears were not far away and I managed to summon up enough pride not to shed one.

Mrs Pearson kept coming to where we were sitting, offering soft drinks, cakes, but I'm sure she felt the strain of not being able to talk about my school or Sophia's.

Just before I left, Sophia handed me a calendar.

'If you hang it in your room you can see the day when I'll be back marked,' she told me. 'I'll write to you every week and you can write back. You will, won't you?'

I swallowed hard, trying to make the lump in my throat dissolve.

'Of course I will,' I told her.

And then it was time for me to go home. And if I thought my day could not get worse, I was wrong.

My therapist waited patiently while I set my shoulders back, took a deep breath and resumed my story. I'm sure she knew what was coming.

'He came into my room that night. It was the first time since the teacher had been to the house. I had known all evening that he would. I could feel his eyes on me, mocking me. He must have known then that there was now no possibility of me confiding in the Pearsons. He had just been biding his time to when there was no one left I could turn to.

'He had seen me when I arrived back from Sophia's, saw by the way I raced upstairs that I was upset. It was my mother who called me down and told me my father was going out to buy us all fish and chips and ordered me to set the plates out and lay the table. Neither of them asked what was wrong, which is another reason why I believed that Mrs Pearson had at some stage informed them of the fact that she had enrolled Sophia in a boarding school.

'When my father returned, he had for once bought generous portions for all of us. We could all, he told us, go into the sitting room and watch television afterwards, because he was taking my mother out for the evening. A remark that placed smiles on my brothers' faces and dread on mine.

'I knew what that meant. He would ply her with enough gin so that when they returned, he could leave her snoring on the settee and then visit me. And if I had any doubts as to what his intentions were, his good humour and broad smile dismissed them. My mother might have made herself believe that he was in a good mood because business had put some money in his pocket, enough at least to treat us all and take her down to the pub, but I was not fooled.

'God,' I told my therapist, 'he looked so bloody smug that I just wanted to scream. I could feel his eyes on me all the time we sat at that table.

'That evening, I could not concentrate on watching television – I don't think I was even aware of what was on.

Instead it was the clock my eyes were fixed on and the sound of it ticking away the minutes until my father returned that I listened to.

'We knew not to stay up too late for they would not want us downstairs when they arrived back. And at ten o'clock we all disappeared upstairs. I pulled on my nightdress, curled up in bed, with my hands clenched. There was no point trying to sleep for he would have no qualms about waking me. Lying there, I felt the chill of loneliness. My new clothes were hanging neatly on the back of the door. My gym clothes were folded up inside a new blue bag. My pencils lay in a shiny wooden box and a silver-coloured fountain pen was clipped to a pocket inside my brand new satchel: I was ready for school. I sneered at the thoughts I had allowed into my head earlier that this time I would not look different, that I might feel more like I belonged. For however much I looked the same as my peers on the outside, I was never going to be the same on the inside.

'I heard the front door opening; his voice loud and hearty, her words slurred with drink. I listened as he went into the kitchen to fetch another drink – he did not want her coming up yet, he wanted to leave her snoring on the settee. It did not take long before I heard the creak of the stairs as he stealthily climbed them. I lay there counting his steps: just eight more would bring him to my door.

'"Keep still," I told myself, "keep very still. Breathe deeply, he will think you are asleep." A vain hope, I knew. Then he was in the room. My closed eyes might have obscured the shape of his body but I could smell tobacco and the fumes of alcohol before his hand reached down and stroked my head.

"I thought my girl might be lonely," he said in a whisper and I caught the satisfaction in his voice as he murmured those words.

'I heard the sound of his zip being undone, felt the bed sag as he climbed in behind me. His arms went around my body and without opening my eyes I could see that black spider hovering over my stomach again.

'There was little difference to what he did that night than all the other times. First, a fumbled cuddle and all the time he whispered that "I was his special girl". I just lay there stiff and unresponsive, just waited for what was inevitably going to happen. His breath rasped in my ear and when I heard it quicken, I knew that he was ready to climb on top of me. I was right; he flipped me over onto my back as effortlessly as though I were a rag doll.

'It was over quickly. A few thrusts, a groan and then he got out of my bed. Then he did as he had done every time, passed me a rag to clean myself.

'He stood there as I obeyed. Then, assured that the evidence of a sin he believed my mother was unaware of was wiped away, he took the piece of cloth from me and left. And when he was gone I lay dry-eyed, staring at the disguise of normality that hung on the back of my door; new school clothes that no longer gave me pleasure.'

'And two days after that you started school. What was it like for you there?'

'I hated it. Even though the new uniform made me more confident, I seemed to be the only girl there who did not have a friend to chat to during our breaks; I would even have welcomed Jimmy, but he had to wait another two years before changing schools. Not being a child who had the confidence to start a conversation, I would instead try and make myself invisible by standing in corners and spending as much time as I could in the lavatories.

'At lunchtime I would take my tray to the nearest table. When it filled up around me, all I could hear was conversation that I found impossible to be part of – I mean I could not find anything to add to it that would make me sound interesting. There they were, my fellow classmates, chatting about programmes they had seen on television that I had not been allowed to watch. On Fridays, there was always talk about their weekend plans. On Monday, of course, they vied with each other in telling what it was they had done over those two days. I could never think of one thing to say that would make them take notice of me.

'Well,' I added dryly to my therapist, 'apart from telling them about my father coming into my room at night, that is. And there were times I was almost tempted. They were just so complacent about their happy little lives! But of course that would not have made me any friends – just the opposite, I suspect – so I remained silent.'

'Most probably, that was for the best,' said my therapist with a deadpan expression.

'I think they saw me as a mousy little thing – boring, but harmless – and just ignored me.'

'And Ben? How was he there?'

'Ben,' and as I said his name I felt a wave of sadness, 'I think he was very unhappy but all I could see then was that he made things much worse for me. Also, whereas once I had felt protective towards him, when I started that school I no longer did.'

'Why was that?'

'He changed after that horrible day when my father destroyed those things that he loved and I did not like how he had become.'

'Yes, you have told me that the events of that Saturday had a lasting effect, not just on you, but on both your brothers as well. Can you tell me more about that?'

I thought for a moment, trying to find the right words.

'With Jimmy, I don't think he ever stopped being afraid of our father after that. But it was not long after that Saturday that he became nervous around Ben also. His brother was not someone he had ever tried to be close to – well, you see, Ben was just there. Slow and clumsy he might have been, but before that day he was always very sweet-natured. Even when the boys at school mimicked his walk and laughed at him, he never reacted.'

'And that changed?'

'Yes, not overnight, but it did not take long.'

'And did you become frightened by him?'

'Not as much as Jimmy, but then I was closer to Ben in age. But I was very wary of him all right.

'I had believed, ever since he was given the task of walking home, first with me and then when Jimmy started school, with both of us, that he took pride in being our big brother. And I, understanding that the responsibility was important to him, played up to that image longer than I needed to.'

'So how did he change?'

'He started to show an aggressive streak that I had never ever seen before. After that day I had felt there was something really wrong with him; it was certainly more than just being slow. I knew he was absolutely traumatised by what had happened. The only way I can describe what he was like then is he sort of retreated into himself. There were no smiles, no occasional bursts of laughter, just blank looks before he turned away from us. Though I suppose then Jimmy and I just put it down to Ben being Ben.

'I had always known he was different – Jimmy and I both accepted that. Even if sometimes the way he was caused us embarrassment, he was still our brother. And both of us hated the way he was picked on. But as I said, he had never been nasty to us. When I gave him those presents from Mrs Pearson he hugged me so tight; he was just grateful. Even a few words of praise from my grandparents would put a wide smile on his face – it took so little to make him happy. I don't think my grandparents were aware of just how frightened he was of my father. I noticed that neither of my parents called him names like "moron" or "spastic" when they visited, although no sooner had the door shut behind them than my father had no qualms in making up for it and I would see all the brightness that my grandparents' visit had put on Ben's face fade away before he took himself despondently to his room. I felt grateful to Mrs Pearson then; at least he had his jigsaws to occupy himself with.

'You know, my parents were so cruel. I came to recognise the fact that they did not like to see Ben happy. I know that's hard to believe; that anyone would be that vindictive, but I know I'm right. I just can't understand why.

'When I tried to be nice to Ben, my father would give one of his snorts of displeasure and say, "Oh for goodness' sake, Cassie, stop bothering with that moron and help your mother instead!" I wonder if, when he was small, my mother ever placed him in the pram and wheeled him down the road. She might have done when he was a baby but I'm sure as soon as she was told that he was always going to be slow, she stopped. I think she was ashamed that she had produced such a child. I've told you that she had little time for any of us, but there was a real resentment directed towards him. There were times when Ben reminded me of a puppy, one that's forgotten his master kicked him and still comes back, wriggling up for attention. How many times did I see those trusting eyes turned in my mother's direction just hoping for a kind word, a scrap of affection or even a smile? Instead he was snapped at. I saw how much he hurt. He never tried to say anything though, just hunched his shoulders and slunk away. But he still kept trying. It was so sad to see, I really felt for him. He was so lonely and so pitiful.'

'You said after the toy incident he began to show some aggression. Who was that towards?'

'I think it was only towards Jimmy and me. I never heard that he had done anything to any other child.'

'And the change that took place in him, you say it was a gradual one?'

'Yes, and at first I did not really take much notice. I suppose I was too wrapped up in my own affairs. First, with the time I was spending with Sophia and then feeling sorry for myself when I knew about her leaving. Let's just say I should have started noticing more, but I was too immersed in my own misery.'

'I think that was understandable, Cassie. You knew you were going to miss your friend and from what you have told me you could not see anything going right in your life.'

'Yes, that about sums it up. I missed Sophia, my older brother was messed-up and my father was back to feeling he owned me. If I had given him a scare by talking to the teacher he was well and truly over it. He was always asking me to bring tea out to his shed. Sometimes that was all he wanted, other times it wasn't. And it was the not knowing which it would be that made me nervous. Sometimes he would just tell me to put his mug down and I could let the tension out of my body, but other times those grimy hands of his would snake under my clothes while I breathed in the combined stink of him and that shed.'

So no, I hadn't taken much notice of Ben, but I certainly had become aware of the changes when I walked through the school gates. It was not just him, but also the way others acted around him.

There was now something aggressive about the way he looked. Hard to put a finger on what it was exactly, but it was there all right. I noticed almost straight away that the other pupils tried to give him as wide a berth as possible.

When we were in the playground no one jeered or teased him as they had done in Juniors. Nor did the younger ones walk behind him imitating his strange loping walk, as had often happened before. And that took me by surprise. As it did when I stood next to him and suddenly noticed how much he had grown – he seemed to tower over me and I was tall for my age. And not only had he shot up in height, but his body had really filled out as well. Evidently he had been spending as much time as possible in the school gym. Whatever exercises he had been doing had certainly worked. His muscles were practically bulging through his jumper. He was certainly no longer puny little Ben. It seemed as though overnight he had become bigger and stronger than the bullies who once mocked him.

But it was not only his physique that made him appear different, his facial expressions were also altered. No longer did he look hopeful or pleading. There wasn't even a hint of timidity there. In fact, his face was almost expressionless, a blank mask that covered any emotion he felt. A few years at secondary school might not have taught him much in the way of the Three Rs, but it had taught him to hide his hurt. I have to say though that the senior school did turn out to be a bit better for him than the junior one. Instead of having to sit with classmates of his own age and struggle with the lessons in front of them, he was placed in a special class for children who found learning difficult. I heard he was the slowest one of the pupils there, but I don't think the teachers had much interest in that class anyhow. They didn't expect the kids in there to learn much, so he was left pretty much alone.

*

'Unfortunately, that happened then,' my therapist observed. 'Thank goodness there has been a lot of progress in the education system. Children like your brother are recognised as having special needs. And now they are given a lot more help.'

'I know, and I think that if he had been at a school where he was taught some social skills and made to feel more confident, the kind sweet boy he had been would not have vanished.'

'Did you see much of him at school?'

'Not really, but I still walked home with him. But it was not long before he made me feel nervous. Once, when my shoelace had come undone and I asked him to wait, he grabbed my arm hard and then strolled off. I just put that down to uncharacteristic bad temper. But soon after, acts of real spite started happening. That was something I had not been expecting. The first time he pinched me hard just above my elbow, I rubbed my arm and told him that it had hurt.'

CHAPTER EIGHTEEN

I never thought he meant to cause me pain, just that he had misjudged his strength. And I thought he would apologise, but no, instead he giggled. It was a high unpleasant sound that I had not heard him make before. That was the start of him frequently pinching and nipping me, and it did not take him long before he started picking on Jimmy as well. His eyes would dart around and when he thought no one was looking, he would sneak up behind his brother and pinch him hard and then giggle when Jimmy yelped in pain. No, he was no longer the brother I had known was slow, but in a way, looked up to.

I could have made excuses that I had to stay to see a teacher or anything else that came into my head so I could walk back alone, but I hadn't the heart to. I wished we could have walked with some of my classmates who lived on the estate, but they never asked us. I was Ben's sister, and even if they had accepted me, they never would him.

Chapter Nineteen

'Have you some good memories about your time at the school?' asked my therapist.

'Well, yes. When I had been there for a while I received praise from the gym teacher. At last I had been told I was good at something.

'"Cassie, you are the fastest runner here," she told me and I can't tell you how happy that bit of praise made me feel. I felt even happier when she told me that I was to be in the relay team. There were another three girls she had chosen. Our names were called out and suddenly I was part of a team.

'"You will be competing on sports day," she told us and at those words I felt so excited. I really thought that finally I was part of something.

'But it didn't last. Feeling happy like that, it all got ruined. I mean, it should have been the beginning of me enjoying being at the school, but it wasn't. And that was all because of my father. It was then, after that sports day, that I began to really hate him.'

As thoughts about that day came into my mind, I realised my hands were clenched so tightly that my nails were digging into the palms.

'Take a deep breath, Cassie, and start with telling me what you did after you were chosen for the team,' my therapist said soothingly.

'Practised,' I said with a faint smile. 'In fact, our group began practising almost straight away. And over the weeks leading up to sports day I felt a growing comradeship beginning to blossom between us. I was to be the first runner and speed was important.

'I was so determined to increase my pace that whatever the weather was like, I made myself run around the track at least four times every day.

'When I told my grandmother that I was to take part in the race she took me shopping again. Running shoes, shorts and a new white tee shirt were bought on that expedition. At last, I felt I could hold my head up high.

'The night before sports day I lay in bed dreaming of us winning. I so wanted to hear the applause and have a rosette pinned on me in front of everyone.

'My parents had been invited and in a way I half-hoped they would come. Surely, if they saw me achieving something they would be proud of me. I think I wanted that more than I ever admitted. Silly, wasn't it? I mean, I should have known better.'

'No, Cassie. Wanting your parents to praise you for something is normal. So what happened?'

'Well, when I asked my mother if they were coming her answer was "What? Just to see a load of children running around a field? Anyhow, your father's got some work on and I've got better things to do with my time, thank you."

'I suppose I was hardly surprised, just a bit disappointed, but I refused to let it upset me. I did think though, why couldn't she just pretend for once that I was of some importance to her? I think it was then that I decided if she had no time for me, I had none for her. The difference was that over the years I managed to hide my feelings while she did little to mask hers.

'The day I had been looking forward to finally arrived. Sunlight was streaming through my window when I awoke. Bedclothes were thrown off, and out of my window I saw a clear blue sky.

'I remember looking in the mirror once I was dressed. Instead of the old mousy me, I saw a different girl. Still tanned from the summer holidays, I looked fit and confident. I felt happy and it showed. I remember thinking that it was going to be a perfect day, even if I was the only pupil in any of the races whose parents were not present.

'It was when I went into the kitchen that I should have known not everything was going to go as I had planned. My father, dressed in his usual working clothes, was sitting at the table and a broad smile came in my direction, a smile I did not trust.

'"I can see you're ready for the big day, Cassie," he said, before mentioning that he had to take a car he had fixed for a run. "I'll take you to the school," he added. "No need for you to walk there, I've got to pass it."

'My heart sank: he was not someone I wanted to spend time with before the race. Nor, I realised, did I want to be seen with him.

'I had noticed that the other fathers, even the ones on our estate, wore sports jackets and decent trousers whenever they came to the school whereas my father would be wearing his usual work clothes, smeared with oil stains, and driving an old banger.

'He told me to swallow some breakfast and that he wanted to leave a bit earlier: he had something to drop off on the way.

'I did not feel suspicious, just relieved he would have dropped me off before my classmates arrived. It was only once we had driven out of the estate and I felt his hand on my knee that I started to question what his real motive had been in offering me a lift.

'"My, Cassie, you are looking very nice today. Quite the little lady, aren't you? All dressed up in your sports gear." At those words I remember feeling as though lumps of ice were sliding down my back. And all I could think was, "Please don't start anything today." As though reading my silent prayer he chuckled, and the sentence he had used on me so many times before came out of his mouth: "Don't be getting ideas, Cassie. You've still got time for your old man, haven't you?" I knew then what he had in mind. Even so I managed to stutter "Yes," for the fact was that just his voice and that hand on my leg had already reduced me to the frightened six-year-old I had been when he first touched me.

'His hand tightened while his foot pressed down on the accelerator and I felt panic rising up in me.

'"Dad, I don't want to be late," I pleaded.

'But he just grinned at me and told me that was why we had left early. Then more of his well-worn sentences came in my direction. "Don't you trust me, Cassie?" followed by "If you just do what you are told, you will be nice and early, all right?"

'"Yes," I muttered through clenched teeth to the first one. I was nearly in tears by then. The day was spoilt almost before it had begun. We passed the school and with a sickening feeling I guessed where he was taking me.

'I was right; he turned down a road little more than a lane and then stopped the car near the woods. Not the part where I had seen families and dogs walking when he had left Jimmy and me, but the part where the foliage was thickest and most dense.

'"Nice and quiet here," he said, still with that smirk on his face, "no one about."

'"He can't think of doing it out here," I had thought with horror. I was scared that someone would come and imagined a leering face peering through the window and seeing my humiliation.

'"Now, Cassie, you know what to do," and saying that, he moved his seat back, unzipped his trousers and released that loathsome red thing, which in anticipation of feeling my hands on it, was already swollen. His voice, giving me instructions, wormed its way into my head, setting off tremors of fear, as well as filling me with disgust and self-loathing.'

I glanced at my therapist then: 'I know I should have screamed "No," or "Stop," or anything that would have shocked him enough to make that red thing shrivel up. But no, as usual, I found it impossible to disobey him. So I let his hand cover mine and my fingers curled round that thing and I rubbed it as he told me to. And every time I moved my hand I hated myself even more than I hated him. I mean, why was I just so weak?'

'You were what age then?'

'Somewhere around 12.'

'You were still a child, Cassie, and he had programmed you over the years to do exactly what he told you. What did happen at the sports day?'

Gratefully, I realised her question was a way to deflect my thoughts and make me think of something more positive.

'We still won,' I said and a smile crossed not just my face as I said that but my therapist's too.

'Not so weak then, Cassie!'

'I was angry. No, more than angry – I was full of rage. I was not going to let him reduce me to a complete wimp and he didn't, not that day anyhow.

'I had never run so fast. Rage lent me wings. And I could hear the cheers, and I got that rosette.'

'And did your life at home improve?'

'Not after I fell pregnant.'

Chapter Twenty

My therapist told me that although she understood there were some memories that affected me more than others, she still wanted us to discuss them in order. So I knew what she wanted to talk about next. Not my pregnancy, not my adult years, but my early teenage ones when Sophia had returned from her first term at school.

And again I took out my notebook and made more notes while I travelled back in time to when I was a 12-year-old, eagerly counting down the days to the Christmas holidays. Sophia had kept her promise and written to me every week. At first her letters told me how much she missed both me and her home, but gradually, their content began to change. At first she added descriptions of activities she was fast becoming involved in, and then a little later in the term she wrote about some of the other pupils as well. Every letter ended with her saying she was looking forward to seeing me. I could tell though that not only was she settling into her new school, but she was also enjoying it. The last letter I received before Christmas arrived not long before my own school was due to break for the two-week holiday.

They have dogs here, she wrote, lovely golden Labradors. Well, not exactly here, but the Guide Dogs Training Centre is next to the school. Some are almost qualified guide dogs and they are being introduced to those who will need them when they leave school. And there are younger ones, still puppies almost, that are still being trained. We are learning how to handle them, such as giving the eight commands and how to walk with them. Some of the dogs don't pass their training and those pups are found really good homes. Although I won't need a guide dog when I leave school, I keep asking Mummy if I can take one that has failed its test. They are so adorable, Cassie, and we could walk it in the holidays.

That was followed by a row of Xs.

After I read the letter I realised that she had not given me the date when her term ended. I waited a day, and then took myself off to visit her mother.

It had seemed quite strange walking up that drive without Sophia being at the other end to greet me and I just hoped I would still be welcome. But I needn't have worried. Almost as soon as I rang the bell the door swung open and I was greeted by a smiling Mrs Pearson.

'Cassie! How lovely to see you,' she exclaimed as she ushered me in. 'Now,' she said as soon as we were in the kitchen, 'take a seat and I'll get us both some lemonade and I'm sure you won't say no to a slice of cake. I want to hear all about what you have been doing and how you like your new school.'

And scarcely had I sat down than a slice of thick fruitcake was placed in front of me.

I felt a sharp burst of nostalgia when I pictured what it had been like only a few months earlier when I had allowed myself to believe that I was almost part of the family. But still, I was pleased that I was able to respond to her questions, about my time at school, with some degree of pride by telling her I was doing well in sports and even some of my drawings had been hung up in the art classroom.

'Well, you and Sophia will certainly have lots to tell each other when she comes home,' she said brightly.

Of course all I wanted to hear was when Sophia was arriving and that I was invited round the same day and hopefully this time I could sleep over. Then I would be there to greet her and we could spend hours telling each other about what we had been doing over the last few months.

That, I soon realised, was not going to happen.

'We are going to drive down to fetch her,' Mrs Pearson quickly told me when I asked. 'We will stay overnight and have a family evening. Now,' and here she smiled, 'I am sure both of you are looking forward to meeting up, so do come round on Tuesday. We'll all be back then.'

As I told my therapist about that day I looked over at her, trying to gauge her opinion on what I was about to say.

'I felt then that she was already controlling the amount of time we were to spend together. Not that she was anything but friendly; why, she even hugged me when I left, but still that was what I felt.'

My therapist made no comment at this stage on my thoughts. 'And what was it like when you met?' was all she asked.

'I found I did not have as much to tell her as I had thought. Not that she seemed to notice. She hardly stopped talking about the school, the teachers, the puppies and the new friends she had made. It's very difficult, isn't it, to try and show an interest in people you have never met, especially,' and I smiled a little wryly, 'when you are 12 and feeling both insecure and jealous?'

I then looked back down at my notes and transported myself back to that day. Amy was a name Sophia kept bringing up and over the course of the day it was one that before too long began to irritate me.

'She has hair the same colour as me,' Sophia told me.

'No,' she said somewhat wistfully to my question asking whether they sat together in class, for she said Amy was a year older. Amy's parents lived nearby so she did not have to board, but she did stay at school to do her homework. Then, as I listened to her, my hands clenched with annoyance as Sophia told me how much she enjoyed visiting her new friend's home.

'She has a Labrador puppy, just like the one I want,' she added. 'Oh I wish you could meet her, you would really like her, Cassie.'

A comment that took all my willpower not to reply by saying, 'No, I wouldn't!'

'You know,' I said to my therapist, when I reached that part, 'I started feeling really miserable. I had so looked forward to seeing her and all she could do was talk about Amy and what a good time she had been having. She hardly asked me any questions about what I had been doing over the weeks since we had last seen each other. And as for Amy, I felt I could hardly compete there. She had a nice family and a dog. I remember I just sat there saying very little and gritting my teeth with frustration. And then, to make matters worse, she started telling me about another achievement.'

And I described to my therapist how Sophia, her cheeks pink with barely suppressed excitement, told me that when she returned to her school, she was going to be able to cycle.

'How are you going to do that?' my resentful 12-year-old self asked, for that was one of the things she had told me with great sadness that she would never be able to do.

Oblivious to my lack of enthusiasm, she told me that Amy, or rather Amy's family, had arranged it.

'They use tandems,' she explained, 'You know, Cassie, those funny two-seater bicycles. The sighted person sits at the front. Well, it would hardly be a good idea if the blind one did,' she added, amidst gales of laughter at that thought. 'Anyhow, I went out with them once. Amy lent me her bicycle and, oh Cassie, it was so wonderful! I'm lucky I've grown this year, so that my legs are long enough to reach the pedals. So guess what I'm getting for Christmas. I chose it when Mummy and Daddy came down to collect me, it's a lovely shade of blue. It's been delivered to the school, so it will be waiting for me when I get back. I think Mummy is almost as pleased with it as I am. She is just so happy that I am starting to have the same hobbies as everyone else.'

'If you brought it here, I could cycle at the front,' I said, hoping that Mrs Pearson would hear me and chip in with an 'Oh, what a good idea!'

'Mummy, what do you think?' asked Sophia, seemingly oblivious to the fact that as her mother was only a few feet away from where we were sitting, she must have heard my remark and chosen to ignore it.

'Maybe when you and Cassie are a little older,' she answered after a slight pause. I understood that she meant that she had little faith in my ability to be in charge of a two-seater bicycle when her daughter was on the back.

Mrs Pearson clearly wanted the subject changed from cycling and, interrupting Sophia's next flow of conversation, said, 'Now, Sophia, let Cassie get a word in. I'm sure she wants to tell you about being selected to run in the relay team and how she won the hundred yards race.' In fact I did not want to remember that sports day at all and anyhow, I thought, it would all sound very tame compared to Sophia's conversation. I just wished I could think of something exciting to tell her. But there was very little I could contribute for since she had left I had not made even one real friend. There were no invites to other girls' houses I could talk about. No exciting hobbies

I had taken up. It was the friendship with Sophia I wanted to cling to, but when I left the house that day I felt completely excluded from her new life.

'And how was the rest of the holiday?' my therapist asked, still without making any comments.

'I think "strained" would be the right word to describe it. All the time I was aware that, although she enjoyed being at home, she was looking forward to getting back to school and seeing her new friends. Also, which was even worse, I had begun to realise that we had nothing much in common to talk about any more.'

'Cassie, I understand that would have been hurtful, but in a way it had little to do with you. I think, for her, it was that she was no longer feeling different. For the first time she was comfortable around her own age group. And that must have been exciting for her. But then you, aged only 12 years old, could not have understood that.'

'Yes, I think I can see what you mean. I suppose I was just too immature to be pleased for her.'

'I think "too young" is a better expression to use, Cassie.'

'I did spend a bit more time with her. Really, it was much the same as the year before. It was the day before Christmas Eve – a nice tea and presents to take home. There were little ones for my brothers as well.

'I only saw her once more after that. She and her parents were visiting the cousins on the way back to school. Hugs were given, promises to write made and the words "See you next holidays" uttered. That was the last time I saw her.'

'What happened?'

'They moved. Mrs Pearson did the right thing – came to meet me after school, took me to a cafe and explained that they were leaving the area a week later. It was only after she had gone that I realised she had not given me their new address: the only one I had was Sophia's school.

'She and I continued to write to each other for a couple of months. Each time a letter fell onto the mat and I saw her handwriting, I hoped it would be an invitation for me to visit. It never was. Instead, in the last letter I read, she told me she was spending the summer holidays with Amy.

'That letter I did not reply to.

'She sent a couple of postcards that summer.

'I tore them up.

'She wrote one more time, a letter I never bothered to open. After that I never heard from them again.'

'Cassie, I think from what you have told me that you are right, in that Mrs Pearson was trying to wean her daughter off her dependence on you. She wanted Sophia to have more than one friend. That's natural. As well as the fact that she wanted her daughter to gain confidence in coping with her disability, which that school clearly gave her. She would not have wanted Sophia disliking her time at school. That would have made her feel that in a way she was being punished because she had bad eyesight. And of course Mrs Pearson would have put her daughter's well-being over everything. Which does not mean that, at the time, she was not fond of you. Can you see that?'

'I guess so. Maybe.'

'So all these years later, do you still think that when you saw the teacher talking to Mrs Pearson it was not about Sophia's schoolwork or the decision she and her husband had come to, but about you? And that is the reason you were not invited to the house quite so often?'

'Yes.'

'All right, Cassie, let's look at this in a different way. Have you considered that there might have been a quite innocent explanation as to why Mrs Pearson did not invite you to stay over during those summer holidays?'

'What other explanation could there be?'

'Well, she and Sophia had agreed not to tell you about her leaving until the end of the holiday. So they must have discussed it, mustn't they? She appears to have been the sort of mother who wanted her daughter to form her own opinions. Then jointly, they might have decided not just what was best for them, but for you as well. I'm sure, even if Sophia wasn't, that Mrs Pearson was aware of just how upset you were going to be. And you have told me more than once that she was a kind woman. Maybe it's as simple as that: she wanted both you and her daughter to enjoy that summer holiday. After all, it could not have been easy for Sophia either. Have you ever considered that?'

I thought for a moment.

'No, not really. I believed it as a child and it's got stuck in my mind as being the case.'

'As you say, that belief became stuck in your mind and you have never relooked at it. What I am trying to show you,

Cassie, is that it is important to have good memories. So try and look at that time from a different perspective. If you can do that, you might find that without the veneer of tarnish you have given them, those memories will become ones you can take out and enjoy.

'Another point, do you remember saying that by not confiding in Mrs Pearson, you missed an opportunity? So what do you think she might have done if you had?'

'I think she would have either gone to the Headmistress or social services. But I am certain that if I had told her everything, I would never have been welcomed in their home again. Good, caring parents do not want their children to mix with ones who have been sexually abused.'

'What makes you think that?'

'I put my beliefs to the test once. I asked several mothers what they would do if their child's best friend's father were convicted of abusing her. And do you know the answer four out of the five gave me?'

My therapist was silent; I suspected she knew the answer.

'They said they might feel sorry for the child, but they would not want her mixing with their children. They would not even want such a child in the same school as theirs. A child like that could be too damaged to be a suitable playmate. However awful it must have been, they had their own children to think of.'

'And the fifth woman?'

'She was a kind woman, so she took her time thinking about it before she replied. She said that not wanting a child to be punished for something that was not their fault, she would allow her in the house. But she would make sure that she was always present when the children were together. The other point she made,' and I smiled at my therapist then, 'was that it would have been better if the child's mother had taken her away. Gone somewhere different, where no one knew about their past. Because once other parents were made aware of the child's history, they would be faced with making decisions. So I still think that is exactly what Mrs Pearson did.'

Of course I don't know, and I never will now, but that is what I believe.

Chapter Twenty-One

My voice trembled slightly as I told my therapist just how bleak my teenage years had been. Those years, when raging hormones change the shape of young girls' bodies and fill their daydreams with fairy tales of handsome Mr Right, wedding dresses, motherhood and their own pretty houses, were not the same as the ones I had. My ambition was to escape from home, to move away, to go anywhere my father could no longer find me. Yes, I wanted a place of my own with a wardrobe full of clothes I liked and a circle of friends who in my imagination dropped by daily so we could drink coffee and laugh together. Although I had no clear idea of how that was going to happen, I still went to sleep dreaming of it. But when I awoke, unlike my peers, it was not the cloak of optimism that draped itself carelessly around my shoulders, but the one of loneliness and despair that covered mine.

It was a period of my life that I had no wish to revisit. Just the thought of what happened then is enough to make me say, 'No! No, I don't want to talk about it.' For even all these years later those memories of how it had been for my younger self still have the power to hurt.

As I entered my teens, like other girls of my age I started to see the signs that my body was beginning to change shape. And so did my mother's attitude to me. I heard my classmates, amidst girlish giggles, either talking about being measured for teenage bras, when their mothers took them on shopping trips, or chattering incessantly about boys and pop stars; subjects that held little or no interest for me. I had few memories of my mother ever being anything but impatient or indifferent to any needs I might have, be they physical or emotional. But as I grew taller and my body began to develop, there were more than the usual caustic remarks and dirty looks coming in my direction.

From the moment I had my first period I was made to feel that, for some reason I could not fathom out then, my mother's indifference changed to what seemed like a positive dislike for me. Not only that, there was a tension in the house that was even worse than usual. I could feel my father's eyes on me constantly and my mother watching him.

When I looked in the mirror and saw a teenage girl grown tall for her age, I did not see the pretty teenager that people told me I was growing into. Despite my large hazel eyes and long shapely legs, I did not believe those compliments, for I felt too grubby on the inside to feel at all good about myself.

Unlike my contemporaries, who took a positively gleeful delight in their bodies telling them that they were fast approaching adulthood, I hated the way mine was changing. It was also becoming increasingly clear to me that for once my mother and I had the same opinion. I tried as best I could to disguise the fact that my breasts were growing; I put on tight vests under my shirts and jumpers in the hope that I would appear flatter. Even so, I still felt self-conscious.

When my mother and I walked to the shops together (not for any mother-and-daughter bonding, but so that I could carry her shopping bags), I cringed with embarrassment when I heard wolf whistles. They were, I had quickly learnt, sounds that enraged my mother when they were directed at me and not her.

Each time it happened she would wait until we were well out of earshot before, with her eyes darkened with rage, she would turn to me and spew out a torrent of angry words.

'Oh for heaven's sake, Cassie! What do you think you are doing? I've never been more embarrassed. Looking at those men and encouraging them! You're giving them the wrong idea, aren't you? Well, I certainly hope it's the wrong idea, I never know with you.'

Each time she told me it was my fault my cheeks flamed with both embarrassment and anger at myself for not protesting more. But I knew it was futile to argue with her.

Other girls from my year might shorten their skirts by rolling them up at the waistband the moment they walked through the school gates, and then toss their hair at the same time as giving sideways glances at boys, but I just wanted to be ignored. Unlike the girls in my class, when a boy paid me a compliment I took it as teasing and instead of feeling flattered, I was just embarrassed. I was always convinced that had I acted pleased at receiving the attention, my gullibility would have been laughed at.

It was around then, when the embarrassment of my growing breasts outweighed the dislike of my mother's intolerance, I brought up the subject of needing a brassière. My breasts were still growing, but apart from that I had stayed the same clothes size for a year. However much I tried to wear my loosest jumpers, they all clung to me.

I screwed up my courage and finally asked my mother if she would buy me some bras.

'I really think I need them now,' I told her sheepishly.

An impatient sigh came from her direction, as hearing my question she lowered her magazine and with her lips curled in annoyance, gave me a scornful look.

'I think I'll be the judge of that one, Cassie, seeing as it's me who has to pay for them. Unless of course you have some money saved. Have you?'

'No.'

'Thought not,' she said and the magazine was raised again.

I thought of asking my grandmother as she had been so generous to me over the years. But how could I go to her and say her daughter was refusing to buy me the underclothes I needed?

It was my father who noticed my tight-fitting clothes.

'Here,' he told my mother, peeling off several notes, 'for heaven's sake, take her shopping, Liz. Get her something decent. I don't want any daughter of mine walking around looking no better than a little trollop in the tight clothes she has. Can't you see she's getting to be a big girl in more ways than one?'

Red crept up my mother's neck but she held her temper. Seeing an opportunity, I smiled up at him: 'Dad, could I have some jeans? All the girls have them.'

'No,' he said abruptly, 'girls wearing those jeans are a disgrace, show up everything they've got. No, you'll get a skirt and not one of those too-short ones either, and a couple of jumpers. And,' he added, turning to his wife, 'get her some decent underwear as well.'

Although the word brassière was not mentioned, my mother knew what he meant.

'Mmm, he'll be telling me to buy you something pretty next,' she muttered under her breath and I heard the deep-set resentment behind those words. It was then that I should have realised just what my mother's problem was. Now I was growing, my childhood years were slipping away. I was young; my body firm, while hers was ageing visibly. There was grey in her hair and an addiction to cigarettes had placed deep lines around her eyes and mouth. I realised later it was jealousy she felt, and I was the cause of it.

She did as my father had told her to do, though: she took me shopping that weekend. I could not help comparing it to the day I had spent with my grandmother when after all our purchases had been parcelled up, she had taken me for tea. I knew this was something that was never going to happen with my mother. First stop was a bra shop, one that by the look of it catered for women more in my gran's age group than mine, from where two white 'serviceable', as my mother called them, brassières were bought. I thought then that she couldn't have found anything plainer had she scoured all the shops in that area. We entered another store where, without waiting for my comments, a grey skirt and a couple of jumpers were purchased and then we made our way home.

'Very nice,' was my father's comment when I was told to show them to him.

But they weren't nice: they were designed for a girl younger than me, not one who had entered her teens. But then 'young' was what he wanted me to remain.

It was nearly a year after that brief shopping expedition when my mother's temper at last got the better of her. With its outburst the façade she had hidden behind slid away and I saw the truth. Not only that, she realised that finally I had seen through her pretence of knowing nothing. She might not have wanted to face what her husband was up to when I was a small child and pushed the signs to the back of her mind and refused to think about them. After all, his desires were no threat to her: a man whose interests lie in sexually molesting small helpless children is unlikely to seek the company of a more mature-bodied rival. But I believe that well before my teacher had knocked on the door, she knew. Maybe my mother was never able to admit to herself that what he did was evil. Did she just accept it, feeling secure that he was never going to stray, not when he had fathered exactly what he desired?

My father's complacency at being able to control me made him take risks. Or perhaps it was those risks that added an edge to his enjoyment.

Chapter Twenty-Two

The Saturday I saw through my mother's pretence started out like most weekends. She was going shopping with a friend and leaving me on tea and sandwich duty. I remained in the kitchen for should my father call out, demanding refreshments, his anger was quick to rouse if I did not answer straight away. But that day, not long after the door had closed behind my mother, instead of shouting out his usual request for mugs of tea, he strolled into the kitchen.

'Where's Jimmy?' he asked and to my reply that he had gone round to a friend's house, he grinned smugly. 'Well, what do you know, Cassie? Here we are again with the house all to ourselves. Gives us a nice bit of time together.'

If my mother's attitude towards me had changed and not for the better, so too had my father's. He no longer bothered hiding what it was he wanted, there were no jokes to relax me, no murmuring that I was special. Those days were gone and when I looked into his eyes I saw either a cold flatness or something bordering on contempt.

'You know what to do, Cassie. We don't know how long your mum will be, so get yourself up those stairs.'

And hating myself for obeying him, I docilely did as he asked. At the top of the landing when I moved towards my room he caught hold of my arm. 'Not in there, Cassie, in here,' and he pulled me in the direction of the bedroom he shared with my mother.

'Something different today, it will be nicer. Have more room, won't we?'

'No, Dad, no!' I protested as I took in the room where the pink shiny bedspread was pulled up so that not one crease showed and underneath the pillow, on her side, even though I could not see it, I knew her nightdress lay neatly folded. Everywhere in the room were traces of her. On the back of the door hung the pale blue quilted dressing gown that she pulled on every morning. By the side of the bed sat her slippers, worn down at the back, and on top of the dressing table was a trail of face powder and a tissue with the imprint of her lipstick. This, I felt, was her room, not theirs, and I wanted to get out of it as fast as possible. I might have known that my father coming to my room was wrong, but the feeling of being where my parents slept was far worse – a situation I could see to my disgust was making him even more excited.

I protested again, but to no avail. He just laughed at my discomfort and pushed me onto their double bed.

'Don't be so silly, Cassie. It'll be a lot more comfortable, you'll see,' he said and without wasting any more time, his hands slid under my clothes.

'When was your period?' he asked suddenly and not understanding the reason for this question, I just whispered that it had finished a couple of days earlier.

'Good, won't be needing any rubbers this time then,' was his response as he moved on top of me.

That time he was rougher than usual. His hand went around the back of my neck while the other one wrenched my panties down and within seconds he was thrusting himself into me. I could hear his pants, feel his breath on my face and then I was aware of another sound: a door opening downstairs.

'Mum's back,' I gasped and, horror-stricken, I flew from the room.

Had my mother known when she came back earlier than expected what she would discover? Did she want to confront him? I'll never know. If that was the case, courage deserted her for she appeared to swallow his explanation that he had needed a lie down. My father might have believed that she had accepted his excuse, but I did not. I knew she must have heard my footsteps and known which room they came from, and nervously I waited for something to happen. I was right, for in the end it was not him she tackled, but me.

She must have brooded all day on what she knew had happened, her temper simmering until by the time he left to deliver a car, it had reached boiling point. If for years I had deep down wanted her to discover what he was doing to me, believed she would take my side, I was mistaken. Or perhaps it was because I instinctively knew who she would blame, that was one of the main reasons I played his game of not letting my mother know.

'Have you been in my room, Cassie?' she asked. Not that she waited for an answer for she did not wish to hear one.

It was then that words that even in my worst nightmares I would never have thought to hear from her came spilling from her mouth.

'Listen here, you dirty little slut, that's my husband! He might be your father, but he's mine and you better not forget it. Do you hear me, Cassie?'

I just stared at her, simply unable to comprehend what I was hearing. Was she admitting that she had known all along? That she blamed me and not him? That was simply too much for me to digest. I wanted to run from her, put my hands over my ears to block out the words that she was using as stinging little weapons, but she had not finished with me.

'It won't be long before you can finish school. Shame they raised the leaving age otherwise you could leave here even sooner. Oh, I've watched you over the years, Cassie, make no mistake! You think you've got your father twisted round your little finger, don't you? But let me tell you, he doesn't care a fig for you.'

Much more of the same followed and I tried to move away from her, but her hand gripped my arm, forcing me to look up into a face so mottled with rage that she was scarcely recognisable. Any willpower she was able to muster was focused on not lashing out and hitting me. I think she must have realised that should she start, she would not be able to stop. So instead she lashed out at me verbally.

'Leave me alone,' I managed to shout and from somewhere deep inside of me I found the strength to pull myself away from her and run with my fingers in my ears, trying to block out the sounds of her outrage. I took the stairs two at a time and as I reached my room, deep sobs wracking my body, I flung myself down on the bed.

When I told my therapist about that night I thought I saw something approaching horror in her eyes. She blinked and it was gone.

'What happened after that?' she asked me calmly.

'I stayed in my room all that evening. She did not come near me. But then what could either of us say? I was far too young to understand how a mother could see her daughter as her rival. But that she did, it was as clear as daylight to me.

'That was when I understood with absolute clarity that she would do anything to hold onto my father. Even if he had molested all of his children, she would never have lifted a finger to stop him. After all, if he was going to do it, then it was better he stuck to his own children than went looking elsewhere – I mean, some other kid might have had parents who would have reported him. And that would have brought the police to our door.

'Then as I told you, it couldn't have been more than three months later when I found out I was pregnant. Not that I recognised the signs when I began to vomit – I just thought it was a stomach bug. He must have impregnated me in their marital bed. A bit ironic that, don't you think? It began with just being sick in the mornings but within a week it happened throughout the day – my breasts were sore, my stomach seemed swollen. It was my mother who heard me in the toilet. I must have groaned for she knocked on the door and told me to come out.'

And I closed my eyes for a moment, realising the tension in my body as I sat talking to my therapist. I had brought up the memory of that day that I had tried so hard to bury. I could see my mother, her face grim, as she looked at me accusingly.

'You've been sick in there?' she asked. Not what was wrong or how did I feel, just how long had I been throwing up.

I still thought it was a bug of some sort; I was too naive to know that it might be something different. I had never thought a girl could become pregnant by her father.

'I think I should go to the doctor,' was all I said when I stood in front of her.

'I don't think so, Cassie,' she replied. 'If it's what I think, you're not going anywhere near a doctor or anyone else. Now, lift your jumper, I want to look at your stomach.'

There was a weariness in her tone of voice then.

I did not want her to, but before I could move, her hand was placed on it.

'I thought so! How long did you think you could keep quiet about that? You're pregnant, Cassie,' and as her words sank in, my legs turned to jelly.

She told me to go to the kitchen and then surprised me by making a pot of tea and placing a steaming mug in front of me. For a few minutes she was silent, her eyes never leaving my face as she slowly lit up a cigarette and inhaled deeply.

'Thought you'd have a baby, did you? Not any baby, but *his* baby? When exactly did you think you would tell me?'

But I just sat there still too shocked to speak as my situation slowly dawned on me.

She was looking at me intently and must have seen something in my face that made her voice soften slightly as she said, 'Oh heavens, you didn't know, did you? Not that it makes any difference. You're going to have to get rid of it – you know that, don't you?'

'How?'

'Leave it to me, Cassie. Who saw you being sick at school?'

'Just one of the other girls.'

'And what did you tell her?'

'That I thought I had some sort of stomach bug.'

'And that's all?'

'Yes.'

'All right, we'll stick to that story.'

My mother told me she would send a message to the school saying I had a nasty bout of gastric flu. She was very firm that I was to stay in my room because my brothers had to believe the same story.

I don't know what they were or where she got them from, but that evening she gave me some pills to take.

'I've run a bath for you,' she told me. 'It's hot, but that will help the pills work.'

'What happens if they don't?'

'There are other ways. You're certainly not having that brat here, Cassie. So take the pills and get in the bath.'

I was terrified of doing as she told me; I had no idea of what was going to happen to me. But my fear lent me some courage.

'I don't want to. You can't make me,' I blurted out.

What she said next made my blood run cold.

'If you don't get rid of it, Cassie, just think who will be cutting the birth cord: it will be me. You, all alone with me, and I will be holding a very sharp knife. That's a monster inside you. And we both know who put it there, don't we? It would make Ben look normal. No, it will never draw breath, even if I have to see to it myself. Now do you understand? We both know why you can't go to the doctor. Nor are you ever going to tell anyone about this. If you think you're in trouble now, it's nothing compared to what would happen if you did. You've broken all kinds of laws, you have. Sleeping with your daddy! Disgusting, you are. And don't tell me he forced you. You've not done anything to stop it, have you? Been going on for years, hasn't it? And did you ever come to me? No, of course you didn't! So stop with the innocent act.'

'Looking back,' I said to my therapist, 'I can see now that it was fear, not anger that was fuelling her venom. I mean, one moment she seemed as though she wanted to help me, the next that she wished I had never been born.'

'I'm sure,' replied my therapist, 'that she was very scared, Cassie. She would have known just how bad the consequences of not just what he had done, but what she was persuading you to do as well, could have been.'

'Not much wonder that's why she kept me at home. Imagine if I had been sent to the school nurse. She must have known that if the Head had cross-examined me, I could well have blurted everything out. But of course then I was unaware of what must have been going through her mind, I was just so frightened.'

'So you took the pills?'

'Yes, but to be fair, I think she suddenly realised that it was fear making me resist, for she told me that I was not the only person in our road that'd got rid of an unwanted baby and nothing bad had happened to them.

'That was why she had known who to go to for the pills. So I felt less frightened, then swallowed them and climbed into the bath. She was right, it was hot and when she saw me wincing with the heat, she gave me a drink. "Here, that will help, Cassie," she had said.

'Silly me, I thought she was being kind.

'And can you guess what it was? Gin! So I had my first alcoholic drink when I was sitting in a bath, trying to get rid of a baby.'

'And the pills worked?'

'Yes,' and I tried to describe the searing pain that had woken me during the night and how frightened I had been.

'There was just so much blood,' I told her, 'my thick sanitary towel was saturated. I wanted to call out for help, but was too scared. What would I do if my father came? Instead I staggered to the bathroom and sat on the toilet with my whole body wracked with pain.

'My mother surprised me when she appeared. She told me she would help me, stroked my back as the blood poured out. She even wrung out a facecloth in cold water and placed it on the back on my neck. Eventually, when I was finally able to stand, she put her arm round me and helped me off the toilet and back into my room. But not before I had seen the lumps of something that looked like red jelly floating in the toilet bowl.

'Mum gave me another sanitary towel, placed an old bath towel under my bottom and told me I would bleed for a while once I was lying down in my bed. Then she went downstairs and made me a warm drink, not gin that time. Told me it would help soothe my stomach. And do you know, I was positive that I saw a look of shame cross her face then.'

'You most probably did, Cassie.'

'Maybe, who knows? I mean, I would like to think there was something in her that felt that. I stayed at home for a week. There were no more angry words, it was a sort of truce. She even let me sit with her and watch television and she made me tea and snacks. The sad thing is it was too late. I had longed for her to be motherly when I was young, but now I was just too depressed to notice it.

'I know I should have been relieved that the baby was gone, but I just felt empty. And you know what I remember most about that night now?'

'Tell me, Cassie.'

'My father never called out to ask her what was happening. And I don't believe that he slept all through it. So she must have told him, mustn't she?

'My mother changed after that. There was an air of defeat around her that never left her. And I think it was because my pregnancy had made her his co-conspirer.

'He never mentioned what had happened and for a while did not come near me either. But I felt my mother watching us and knew she was frightened. Perhaps she was afraid of what the outcome would be. For all three of us knew it was not going to stop, not then.

'She might try and guard her house, make it difficult for him, but she could not watch his every movement.'

Chapter Twenty-Three

There was a silence in the room for several seconds after I had finished recounting that part of my story. I felt completely drained. Realising, my therapist gave me an encouraging smile.

'You told me that after your father became aware that his wife knew about his abuse of you, the atmosphere in the house became even more unsettling?' she asked.

'Yes. My father's temper grew worse. There was not one aspect of his life that he was satisfied with. Mind you, his face was worth looking at the day Margaret Thatcher was voted in as leader of the Conservative Party,' I said with a grin as I pictured my father's face reddening with rage when it was announced on the news in 1975. 'The idea of a woman telling the Government what to do made him fly into such an apoplectic rage, I thought the television was going to get thrown out of the window! But apart from that, it was not a happy time. He took to hitting the boys more and hardly spoke a civil word to me.'

'And your mother?'

'She was uncharacteristically quiet. Looking back, I would say she was suffering from depression. Not only

259

was her cover as the unsuspecting wife blown to me, it was blown to her husband and even worse, I think, to her. Knowledge that, up to then, she had denied having was now out in the open – no more pushing it to the back of her mind.

'The tension in the house affected my schoolwork as well. I found it increasingly difficult to concentrate, much to my teachers' annoyance. For what seems a long time my brothers and I lived in a fog of anxiety. We just never knew what might set off our father's temper.'

'Was that when you started self-harming?'

'Yes, I managed to take a razor out of the bathroom. I hid it underneath my mattress.

'You know, you wouldn't think the sight of a thin cut would make anyone feel good, but it did. When I sat holding my arm, watching my skin break and saw that thin line of red, I felt almost euphoric. And then, when I held a tissue under it and watched in fascination as those small droplets of blood fell, it was a sense of freedom that ran through me. I mean, it was my decision how deep I cut. It was even my decision whether I took it one stage further and sliced deep into my wrists. That was something I was in charge of, and at the stage of my life it was the only thing.

'The razor became my secret friend, the sting of pain my release. I hid the cuts well; they were high up on my leg, where they were concealed at all times, even when wearing my gym shorts.'

'Well, elastic bands are a much better idea, Cassie.'

'They are,' I agreed.

'Cassie, after your pregnancy did your father leave you alone or not? You have not told me either way.'

'For a while he did. But then I suppose he thought I had to heal. Not only that, I think it had frightened him a bit. Imagine if those pills hadn't worked. Anyhow, it did not take me long to realise that he was not scared enough. So the answer to your question is that no, that was not the end of it.'

My therapist waited for me to continue.

I dug my nails into my hands. Some of my travels back in time caused wounds that hurt more intensely than others, and this was one of them.

'He started coming into my room very early in the mornings,' I admitted finally. 'The worst part of it was that this was the first time my nights had been calm. Those nightmares that tormented me while I slept had diminished quite a lot. Up to then I had allowed myself to believe that my pregnancy had frightened him enough to think about just what the consequences of it might have been, and I was sound asleep. What I realise now though was that nothing was going to stop him. In his head, he owned me and I was his to do with as he wished.'

As I stated that fact, my mind slid back to the morning I had opened my eyes to find him standing over me. I knew what he wanted, of course I did. I must have felt exactly what a rabbit feels when it gazes into the headlights of a car. Its instincts might be screaming, 'Run, run, you'll get squashed if you don't,' but all four limbs refuse to obey, and it is as though they are paralysed by the glare of the lights.

That was how I felt when I looked up into his eyes.

'I would like my memories to tell me that he placed his hand over my mouth, gagged my screams and shouts of anger, held me down, his strength overcoming my attempts to break away; but they don't. Instead they tell the truth: I was not only mute when he climbed into my bed, but I lay completely still.

'I hardly felt his breath against my face, or was conscious of his smell. His gasps of pleasure barely pierced my ears. I lay inert, my eyes closed, seeing only a white space and feeling nothing.

'When he climbed out of my bed there were no sheets of tissue thrown in my direction, no verbal instructions telling me to clean myself up. Instead out of the corner of my eye I watched as that red thing shrivelled and that piece of rubber fell into his hand. He wrapped it in toilet paper and took it away. I heard the flush of the toilet a few seconds later that told me where it had gone.'

My therapist was silent for a few moments after I described that morning. She had no need to ask if that was the only time he had visited my room before I went to school – she knew the answer. I wondered then if she could visualise the teenage girl climbing out of bed, going to the bathroom, washing, combing her hair and dressing before going downstairs and swallowing breakfast, then picking up her satchel and walking to school.

CHAPTER TWENTY-THREE

'I took pills that night,' I told her. 'Aspirins.'

'How many?'

'Not enough.'

Chapter Twenty-Four

'Cassie, since we started therapy I have tried to get you to think of some of your happy memories, haven't I? I know there were not many in your early life, but there were some. Also, when we talked about Sophia, I think you have come to realise that you were not the reason they moved. It was just a mother putting her daughter's medical condition first.'

'Yes,' I replied thoughtfully.

'I know from your notes that your grandmother died before you were married. I have been aware that you wanted to talk about her. You've mentioned her a lot though and she appears to have been a constant bright light in your life. What I want you to do is think about your memories of her and then we will talk about them.'

'Why?' I asked. 'I mean, she is not part of the reason I am here.'

'I know that, Cassie, but she is a good strong memory. We have discussed that and agreed that it is important to have them.'

I knew by then that my therapist was right. So that evening instead of switching on my television, out came my notebook again. As I scribbled down my recollections I found my mouth turning up at the corners and a feeling of warmth coursed through me.

She was right: I had locked away those memories of the time when age made my grandmother's shoulders stoop and robbed her of her vitality. For too many years I had consigned memories of her last few years to the box marked 'Don't open' and in doing so, I had reduced them to having no more substance than shadows on the wall.

But sitting there with my notebook I understood it was time to take out all those memories, both the happy and the sad ones. My grandmother had been a very special person and a special person deserves her life to be remembered and celebrated. While jotting down my notes, I thought that my children could also come to learn about her through me. In that way she would live on in our minds for many more years to come.

My grandfather died a couple of years before my grandmother. It was some time after his death, when my mind had been too full of my own problems to see her sadness, that I suddenly noticed that my grandmother's eyes, those bright smiling eyes surrounded by laughter-made wrinkles, had dimmed. A shimmer of almost transparent white, so fine but it was there all the same, had begun to cover over the blue. When she stretched out her hand for me to take, I was saddened by the feel of it; once her grip was strong as it guided me, now it was so light, as though under the thinning skin her bones were as fragile as a baby bird's. That was not the image of my grandmother I wished to dwell on. Not the woman who looked at my mother and me helplessly, as over the following months our roles became reversed. But most of us do grow old, something the adult me has to accept.

She died in early October, a month when the plane trees' leaves were turning dark brown before falling, like a thousand fluttering moths, onto rain-slicked grey pavements.

Once I looked back I could see what a mistake I had made in pushing away so much. No, if I want to feel the love she gave me, then I must see that it was given throughout her life.

When I was a child it was her house where I wanted to spend as much time as possible. It couldn't have been more different to my own home, where its patina of dust and smell of reused cooking oil, cigarettes and stale air clung stubbornly to both walls and floors. My grandmother's kitchen, however, like Mrs Pearson's, was the colour of sunshine. There was nothing I enjoyed more than helping her for she not only baked bread, scones and cakes but produced homemade fudge and coconut ice as well. I watched her hands, the knuckles already swollen from the arthritis stalking her limbs, knead pastry, peel potatoes, prepare fruit salad, chop vegetables and slice meat as she prepared one after the other of her delicious and nutritious meals. To my grandmother food was the language of love, and that she had in abundance.

Whether she was busy with her housework, cooking or walking to the shops, there was a visible lightness to her step that belied her advancing age. It was not until I was in the latter part of my teens that I realised she was no longer young. This realisation brought me sadness for it made me begin to understand that she would not always be with me.

My therapist was right: my time with her was full of happy memories. One of my earliest ones is when I was about seven. I had been sent to stay with her – oh, not for ever, which would have delighted me – but to recover from a bout of measles. My mother's excuse for packing me off was that she could not cope with all her children getting ill. And I, wrapped up in a blanket, was driven to my grandmother's, where for two whole weeks I was spoilt to bits.

'Treacle tart, Cassie?' she would say, a twinkle in her eye and a mischievous smile on her lips, when I was feeling sorry for myself. She knew this was my absolute favourite and had baked one as soon as it was agreed I would convalesce at her house.

Her affection was not only reserved for my little brother Jimmy and me. She also showed Ben not just kindness, but understanding as well. 'Little lamb,' she would call him as she ruffled his hair and slipped him some small treat. And for once, feeling singled out but in a kind way, he would lean against her and sigh contentedly.

As picture after picture of my time with my grandmother floats into my mind another image appears, one that is sharp and clear. In it she asks me a question that I do not answer truthfully.

There were shadows under my eyes; I know that because my grandmother had told me. I can see her now, with her glasses pushed on top of her head, for the steam from the cooking had misted them over, observing me carefully.

'What's wrong, Cassie? Is there some problem at home? You're not yourself.'

'No, nothing's wrong, Nan. I'm finding Maths difficult; been getting extra homework, that's all.'

How easily lies, which camouflage our secrets, trip from the tongue.

I glanced at my therapist when I got to that part.

'What I do know though is that I did not imagine that look of relief that crossed her face at my denial.'

'Do you regret not telling her then? I know you have said that one of the reasons you never confided in her, even when she gave you the opportunity, was the fear of not being believed.'

'That might have been part of the reason. But now, no, I don't believe I do. I think having that knowledge would have destroyed her. Especially as not much later my grandfather became seriously ill. Then her attention was focused on caring for the man she had been married to for over 50 years.'

I too grieved for his lack of health. He was the one who had sat me on his knee since I was a toddler. While my nan prepared our meals he read me stories. And he too was kind to both my brothers, though he did single out my older brother for a little bit of extra attention. He took him out fishing and praised him, even if it was only the tiniest of sprats that he had caught. And Ben would look so happy then.

Over the months before he died, he spent much of his time dozing in his chair, until that horrible rattling cough of his woke him.

'Sorry,' he would always say, his hand holding a neatly ironed handkerchief over his mouth, his eyes still watery from his chest's exertions. 'Sorry.' He would wheeze. And my grandmother, seeing him trying to hide the traces of blood in his mucus, would just tap his arm gently.

'No need for that, love, it helps clear your chest,' she would say.

The day he died was the first time I saw tears on my mother's face.

I did not go to the funeral; none of us children did. Even now, I cannot remember my father wearing his black suit, which I know he must have done. I can picture my mother though, dressed head to toe in black, a borrowed hat perched neatly on her head, gleaming polished shoes on her feet and a wad of tissues clutched tightly in her gloved hand. She took no notice of how upset my brothers and I were. Instead she clung to her grief possessively, as though it belonged only to my grandmother and her.

'Why did none of you go to the funeral?' my therapist asked.

'I don't know, they just said we were too young. Maybe that's the truth and maybe they just didn't want to buy us new clothes.'

'And how were you and your grandmother after that?'

'I had expected her to be devastated, but funnily enough, there was a sort of calmness about her. When I visited her, I could feel the silence of his absence but I don't think that is what she felt. There was an imprint of his head on the fabric of the chair where he had sat during his last months. She never got rid of it, nor did she re-cover it when other chairs, less worn, went to the upholsterer. And she told me that she still talked to him. I'm certain that once the curtains were drawn, she sat in the chair next to his, her hand resting on its arm, and told him all about her day.

'When she died, my mother showed me, if not kindness, a faint awareness of how much I was going to miss her. She told me she was not up to going to the house to clear it, but I could go and choose anything I wanted to have.'

'Take anything you want, Cassie, any little trinket that will remind you of her,' were her actual words.

It was a photograph I took, one she must have treasured, for it was there right by her bedside: me and my two brothers on a day when our grandparents had taken us to the beach. There were others too showing much of her life: as a young woman, her marriage and several family photographs taken with my mother when she was a child, standing between her parents. Surprisingly, my mother agreed to me having them all.

I went there one more time, after all her possessions had been taken away. Somehow I needed to feel her presence one last time: but she was gone. Her once cluttered space was stripped to the bones, just a carcass of what it used to be. Standing in the empty rooms I knew she and my grandfather were together.

I turned to my therapist then, a slightly triumphant smile on my lips as I said, 'Do you know what I'm going to do now?'

'No.'

'I'm going to make a scrapbook. I will use those photos to show her life and some pages from these notes you persuaded me to write. She was,' and my smile broadened, 'a very good memory. Thank you.'

Chapter Twenty-Five

I knew that the easy part of my story was coming to an end when after a month of seeing my therapist she asked me to cover the last couple of years at school and tell her how I felt when I left. It would not be too long before I reached the place that I was so reluctant to talk about. I thought about revealing these events with a high degree of anxiety, but then I had to accept that the long-term effects of these actions that I was so unwilling to open up about were the real reason I was there.

She opened our meeting as she normally did with the innocuous remark I was expecting.

'So, let's talk about your last couple of years at school, Cassie.'

'To be honest,' I said, 'there is little to tell you. I just wanted my school days to be over. All I wanted was to get a job and have my own money. And more than anything, I wanted to leave home. Mind you, it did not take me long to realise that the cost of renting, even just a poky bedsitter, was going to be out of my price range. I thought of looking for jobs living in – you know, hotel work or something. But it still wouldn't be my own place; I would not have been independent, there were bound to be rules, so I did not really fancy that.'

'So you stayed at home?'

'Yes, funnily enough, my mother did not seem to mind me staying. She acted as though she had forgotten the threats she had made only a couple of years earlier. But then since that time, she seldom argued with anyone. When I told her I was lining up interviews, all she said was to make sure I was paid enough to chip in to the household bills and for food, which I suppose was her way of telling me I did not have to move out.'

'And your first job?'

'It was in the fruit and vegetable section of one of our local supermarkets. God, it was boring! Mind you, I did see avocados for the first time and some fruit that had never been in our house.

'What I remember most though is being given my very first wage packet. All right, half went to my mother, but the rest was mine. It gave me such a good feeling. Meant I did not have to rely on anyone. I could buy myself exactly what I wanted; even choose what I wanted to wear. It only took a couple more weeks for me to have enough money to go shopping. Clothes were my priority. The first outfit I bought with my own money was a blue denim skirt and a paler blue top. Next stop was Woolworths' make-up counter and finally, I treated myself to a decent haircut. I felt good about myself that day and once home with my purchases safely hidden in my bedroom, I spent some time experimenting with mascara and blusher. It took some concentration, but I got it right in the end. Even though everything had been purchased with my own money and I was contributing to the household, I still carefully wiped my face clean before I went downstairs. I could imagine the remarks it would bring upon my head if I hadn't have done so. After all, I had got enough snide comments about my new hairstyle.

'Anyhow, good as having some money of my own was, it did not stop me being bored with the work. And also, I felt a bit lonely. There were no other girls of my age working on my section. The only conversations I had were with fraught housewives trying to control their children while I was placing their goods in bags. So after about a year, I started job-hunting again. No more shop work, I decided, and found another job in a factory. Not only did it pay better but the workers there were a friendly bunch and some were more my own age. That is where I met my husband. Not that it was love at first sight or anything, he was just one of the small group of workers who took breaks together and went outside to have a smoke.'

'So how did he change from being a work colleague to becoming your boyfriend?'

'Well, a group of us would go out on a Friday night – you know, after work. Most of them were married and shot off home after an hour or so, and then John arrived and joined us. After a few weeks of only spending time together in the group, he asked me if I would like to go with him to the cinema. One of the *Carry On* films was showing the following night. "Be a good laugh," he assured me. I did not really think about it as a date; well, not that first time anyway. Mind you, when he gave me a box of Maltesers, I did begin to wonder.

'He was a perfect gentleman that evening. Walked me home and then blushed when he asked if I would like to do the same thing the following Saturday. It was strange in a way, going out with a boy. He was the first, you see. But what it did was made me feel normal, something I had not felt since I had stopped being part of Sophia's family. And that feeling made such a big difference to me. On those Friday nights out with my workmates, I felt myself laughing and chatting with confidence that had been completely lacking throughout my school days. I took pride in my appearance and received compliments and accepted them without thinking that I was being mocked.

'That was the start of what then was considered a courtship. That's really how it was back then. Very few of us could afford to leave home, most of my friends did not move out until they got married. And when we went out with a boy more than three times, we were considered a couple: "going steady" were the words used. Well, I know the sixties had changed all that for some, but that's how it was in our area anyhow.

'Our third date was a drive in the country. He borrowed a car and took me to a lovely old country pub, where we ate chicken in a basket. We were relaxed together and giggled when he asked me if I thought they did soup in a basket too! Of course you can't get chicken served that way now,' I said with a grin to the therapist, 'unhygienic. I suppose it was, but then, it seemed so sophisticated for a girl like me. So thanks to Brussels nowadays it's chicken and chips on a plate; just not the same, somehow.

'After several months he told me that his mother, a widow, had invited me for Sunday lunch. Well, back then after a few dates and an invite to meet the mother, that only meant one thing, didn't it?' I laughed then at the thought of how things had changed. 'I mean, it would be expected that there would be a few more invites and then after a respectable time, say six months or so, an engagement would follow.'

'And did it?'

'Oh, yes! Though sometimes I wonder if it was his mother that had more influence on my decision than him.'

'Why is that?'

'His mother – June, her name was – made me feel so welcome. She really fussed over me. She was never going to turn into one of those overprotective mothers, where their daughter-in-law can do no right. Plus, this time when I had begun to feel part of a family, I was certain that I was wanted.

'June reminded me a bit of my gran. Not to look at – she was small and wiry with dark hair whereas my gran was comfortably plump with grey hair – but in how she ran her home and her huge kindness. No bought-in cakes for her, she told me. "Cooking is another way of showing love," was one of her sayings when she put something freshly baked onto my plate. And I mean, she would hardly ever let me help her either. I had to fight to give her a hand with the washing up. Not surprising then that I loved eating at her house. I could not help wishing that I had been raised by a mother like her;

one who paid me compliments and hugged me each time I came to the house. So yes, I do think that was one of the reasons I had begun to like being with John. It had not taken long for me to really like feeling part of her family, even when it was only the three of us. After a while other relatives were invited and although I felt that they were summing me up, I also sensed their approval.

'He proposed to me on a Friday. We were in the pub with the usual group of workmates when he took my arm and whispered that he had booked a table at the new Chinese restaurant. Of course I said something silly like it wasn't my birthday, was it? Eating out was unusual for us. Going to a restaurant was looked upon as a "special occasion" treat. He was very conscientious about putting some money aside every week. Wanted to get his own place one day, he had told me. So really, I sort of guessed what was coming next. He asked me to marry him almost as soon as we were seated. Not down-on-one-knee stuff, with a ring in a fancy box, but ...'

And with that I unexpectedly felt a prickling in my throat as I was transported back in time to when a young man with love in his eyes told me he would be honoured if I agreed to become his wife.

'He was just so nice, so sincere,' I told my therapist, 'and look what I did to him.'

As if on cue a tissue was silently passed into my outstretched hand. I gave a deep blow on my nose and lit a cigarette then inhaled deeply before straightening my back and waited for my therapist to speak.

'Cassie,' she said gently, 'we will get to that part of your story soon. I know you don't understand why I am making you tell me everything in sequence, but you will. Now, do you need a few minutes to compose yourself?'

'No, I'm all right. Just those memories, you know.'

'And you said yes to his proposal?' my therapist asked, making sure that I was back on track.

'I did, yes. I can't say I was surprised, though I knew it was expected by our friends and his mum. I thought he would have been sure of my answer but he can't have been. For a smile of such pure happiness lit his face as he reached over the table and squeezed my hand. He ordered us sparkling wine to celebrate. Sweet, it was, and didn't really go with Chinese food, but we didn't care. He told me he hadn't brought a ring with him because he wanted me to choose one myself. "After all, you'll be wearing it for the rest of your life," he had said with a huge beam on his face.

'His next suggestion made me go a bit cold: he wanted to come to my house to collect me before we went into town to the jeweller's. He thought it was time he met my parents, since he was going to be their son-in-law. Something that for him was said quite firmly.'

I had, over the time I had known him, explained that I had problems with my parents. That my mother suffered from depression and my father was overprotective. 'He doesn't really like me having a social life, wants me in at night,' were two of the things I had told him. Plus, I had added that my father would grill him about his job and everything else he could think of. John, being quite a shy man, was easily put off. But those excuses could not work for much longer, I realised then. Getting engaged changed everything. It would certainly mean that our families would have to meet – that certainly was not a nice thought.

That evening I used the excuse that my mother was having one of her bad spells and it would be better if I caught the bus. I knew John felt hurt, but because he wanted both the evening and the following day to be special for me, he reluctantly agreed.

I caught the bus into town as soon as we had finished breakfast and I had helped my mother clear up. If she noticed that I was dressed in my smartest clothes and had taken care with my make-up, she made no comment. Surprisingly, she thanked me for my help. John was waiting at the bus stop for me and after giving me a hug he took my hand and led the way to a shop where the brightly lit windows were full of gold and silver jewellery. In the centre was a display of rings and I gave an involuntary gasp when I spotted the prices.

I wanted to ask him what his budget was; I had no idea how much he could afford. Probably guessing that was what I was thinking, John tactfully pointed out a couple.

'Thought you might like one of those,' he said, and he was right, I liked both of them and said so.

'Well, let's go in and see what they look like on your finger then,' were his next words and he whisked me into the shop, where an attentive salesman rolled out some blue velvet cloth and placed the two rings I had seen in the window on it, as well as several more.

I tried on the two I had already admired and chose one with a central diamond flanked by two smaller ones.

'I'm still wearing it,' I said to my therapist, showing it to her. 'It's a bit tight now, but I can't bring myself to take it off. John didn't want me to give it back, you know, later.'

'And what happened after you left the shop?'

'Well, I think you can imagine that he was just itching to go back to his mother's and show her the ring. Evidently he had told her we were coming round for lunch and he had a surprise for her so I'm sure she knew exactly what that meant. Not that we made any plans then for a wedding; that was something that had to be saved up for. I thought then it would be at least two years before we would get round to that.'

'His mother was pleased, I take it?'

'Yes, she was; couldn't stop smiling.'

'And your parents?'

'My mother tried to look pleased for me, but I think to be honest, what she felt was a mixture of relief that I would at some time in the future be leaving and apprehension of the fact that being engaged meant I had someone to look out for me.

'She never asked if I had told John anything. I suppose she assumed I hadn't for no angry young man had turned up on their doorstep.'

'And your father?'

'He didn't look happy about it at all. Went a bit red in the face, asked what John did for a living and gave a derisive snort when I told him it was factory work. Then he took hold of my hand, looked at the ring and asked sarcastically when I was going to honour their home by bringing my fiancé there for a visit. In fact it was John's mum who came to my rescue there. She invited them over to hers for a "high tea", as she called it.'

'And how was it?'

'Not as bad as I thought it would be. June really did us proud – there were two salads, potato and mixture of different lettuces with tomatoes, a clove-studded ham and a large homemade fruitcake. Nothing shop-bought on that table! Something she knew not to mention as I had told her my mother thought opening a couple of tins was real cooking.

'My father actually wore a suit and he must have scrubbed his hands hard as for once there was no sign of grease or dirt under his nails. My mother was wearing her best dress and her most charming smile.

'When it was time for them to leave, June and my parents said how nice it was to have met. I don't think any of them meant a word of it, though.'

Chapter Twenty-Six

'How long after you got engaged were you married?' my therapist asked.

'A lot quicker than we planned,' I told her ruefully. 'As I said, John was a perfect gentleman, never pushed me to do anything I did not want to. Not that we had many chances to do more than have a bit of a fumble in the car he borrowed and some snogging, of course. I knew he had reached the stage where he wanted more than that, but still he wanted it to be right. On a proper bed was what he had said, not on the back seat of his friend's car.'

He could have suggested doing the same as some of our friends did: buy a cheap wedding ring and go away to a B&B for a weekend or even take a short holiday. After all, I already had my engagement ring, so it was doubtful any landlord would be suspicious. Thankfully that was not something that John agreed with. 'We are going to be married,' he stated, when I had tentatively asked him if that was what he wanted. 'And I'm not going to pretend to be before we actually are.'

I must say I was pretty grateful for his principles and began to think I could put that act off for ages and I might have been able to, had his mother not discovered bingo. Twice a week she went and we had the house to ourselves. I understood, pretty quickly, that my days of not being expected to have sex were coming to an end. Not only that, I would have to pretend I liked it, and I knew I wouldn't. The stroking and kissing was all right, they made me feel loved, but the other ... Well, I decided I would just have to grin and bear it.

John had never asked me any personal questions about ex-boyfriends before we got engaged, but he did want to know if there were others and what I had felt for them.

'What did you tell him when he did ask about that?'

'The truth – I said I had never been serious about anyone before. That he was the first one who had brought out those feelings. There was no need to lie, I was pretty sure that he believed I was a virgin and that was a belief I was determined he would keep. Anyhow, I blame the bingo for bringing our wedding forward. Well, that's better than blaming our youthful carelessness!'

I might have known more than John about sex: however, that was not something I wanted to admit to. Also, whatever had happened between my father and me still did not mean that I knew that much. I had never gone to bed with a boy; in fact, never even come close to it. So there was still some naivety left in me. I knew about condoms and believed that they were the answer to having sex without getting pregnant. Well, that's what I thought then. John did not like wearing them – I doubt if anyone does really. But I actually think it was more that he was embarrassed at having to walk into a chemist and ask for them. Anyhow, desire conquered embarrassment. It did not take long after his mother found her new hobby for him to purchase a couple of packets.

Our next lesson was learning that condoms are not always fool-proof, especially if the man is as inexperienced as John was back then. Let's just say his excitement overruled caution and the next thing I knew, I was pregnant.

It was his mother we confided in, not mine. Luckily for me, the only time she had met my parents she had not formed a warm impression so she did not ask if we had told them, and if so, what they had to say. Instead of strong reprimands expressing her disappointment in us, to my surprise she appeared more delighted than worried. She wanted to be a grandmother, she told us, and even more importantly, she was quite happy not to have to wait for a couple of years – I think her knitting needles were out the following day, she was that keen. She just told us to bring the marriage forward, suggesting that I could move in and once married, we could stay with her until we found our own place.

The following day I told my parents that we had decided to get married. I did not tell them the real reason, just that we did not want to wait any longer. Although my mother gave me more than one searching look, she did not ask any awkward questions. No comment was made either when they were told it was to be a registry office affair. Most probably they were pleased that they would not be expected to fork out for a church. It was a small wedding, just John's mother, a couple of his cousins and my parents. The local pub where we always went after work put on a spread and our friends joined us there.

June gave us a surprise present. She handed an envelope to John with the details of where she had booked us into for a week. My second surprise was that she had involved my mother, who had packed a case for me. Seats on a train were reserved; we would leave straight after our reception. A few hours later, full of wine and food, with confetti clinging to our clothes and the sound of well wishes ringing in our ears, we climbed into the taxi that was to take us to the station.

My married life had begun.

Chapter Twenty-Seven

'And how was your honeymoon?'

'Most of it was lovely. June had not booked us into a hotel, instead she had rented a cottage on a farm. It was all oak beams and doors that no one over six feet could enter without stooping. The couple who owned the farm had been told it was our honeymoon and not only had they filled the tiny living room with vases of wild flowers, they'd also put out a basket filled with fresh fruit and newly baked bread. And when I looked in the fridge I saw they had stocked it with fresh eggs, a large slab of rich yellow cheese and an assortment of cold meats. They'd even placed a bottle of sparkling wine in it.'

'It sounds a perfect place for a honeymoon.'

'I suppose it was; June would have guessed that we would not have been so at ease in a hotel. Nothing more embarrassing than everyone knowing you're newlyweds and wondering how we had spent our nights! The farmer's wife pointed out that, tucked into a corner of the sitting room, there was a picnic basket, a couple of rugs and several cushions, and then they told us that the old car parked outside was for our use. "Lots of beautiful countryside around here for you to explore," she said, handing John a map. They really had thought of everything.

'On our first full day there we made up some sandwiches and picnicked by the river. Watching a family of ducks gliding past and listening to the countryside sounds, I felt so relaxed. That evening we drove to a small pub that was wedged between a general store and the butcher's. Another place with low doors and oak beams, though you could hardly see them for all the brass hanging everywhere. Wouldn't have wanted the job of having to polish them! We had fish and chips for supper and washed it down with half pints of the local beer.

'It was days like that which were the really good part of our honeymoon. It was the nights I did not like. I can hardly blame my husband for being pretty amorous, it was our honeymoon after all. And to be fair, he was not over-demanding and certainly never anything but considerate to the fact I was pregnant. But still, it was just something I wanted to be over.

'I really did like being in the country, though. On one of our walks round the farm I met the farmer's dog, a big black and white collie with trusting brown eyes. I was stroking his head, enjoying the feel of the rasp of his tongue against my arm, when the farmer, looking amused, came over to us. "He's a working dog," he told us, "but Bruno here, well, he seems to think he's a pet sometimes," he added with a friendly grin. He invited John and me to watch them round up the sheep the next morning and when I saw the collie snapping at the sheep's hooves until they went exactly where he wanted, I was amazed at his speed and agility. I could see what the farmer meant by Bruno being a working dog.

'The sad part of that holiday was when the lorry arrived to take away the white curly-haired lambs I had enjoyed watching gambolling in the field. You know, growing up in the city, you never really think of how meat gets on our plates. But I did after I saw those baby lambs going on their last journey. All I could hear for the rest of that day and all through the night was the crying of their mothers. That upset both John and me. Anyhow, let's just say I might not be a vegetarian, but I went off eating lamb after that. Still don't!

'So the honeymoon was a bit mixed. John was very happy with it. He said we must go back to the farm again. "Bring our children," he added with a mischievous smile. And I suppose that was the first time I had thought of "us", I mean him, me and the baby, as a family.'

'And how was it, living with your mother-in-law, once you returned home?'

'Good. She seemed to love having us in her home, even if it did mean we were a bit cramped for space. In fact, I think she was bit disappointed when the council gave us a flat not long before my first baby was born. Our "starter home", John called it. To me though it was my first ever home and I did my best to make it nice. John and I spent the weekends painting walls and doors. And in between I knitted baby clothes and his mother got her sewing machine out and ran up several pairs of curtains. By the time Paul arrived, the place was looking really cosy. A couple of years later, when I was pregnant with Ken, we were able to transfer to our first house.'

'And you were happy?'

'Yes, I was, most of the time. I liked being a mother and looking after my children. Really, I was content to be a stay-at-home mother. My nightmares lessened as well.'

'And then it went wrong?'

'Yes,' I said, 'it did.'

Chapter Twenty-Eight

'Tell me a little about the time when your mother died, Cassie.'

'I suppose I feel some guilt that I never went to see her even when my father told me she really wanted me to visit. He had rung to tell me she was not well. She had asked for me, he insisted – a surprising statement that I somehow found quite difficult to believe. All I understood from a fairly short conversation with him was that she was having bad headaches. Admittedly he sounded worried, saying she was "not herself". All I thought then was that she couldn't be, if she was asking for me. He rang me a few days later and asked me again to visit; this time I have to admit his voice had a real sense of urgency in it.'

'What was your answer then?'

'I said I was busy. Even then I found it difficult to admit that I never wanted to step into that house again, with its history of secrets, misery and fear embedded in the walls. His response was that being busy was not a good excuse and he questioned why I would not visit. He said that he would go out, if it was him I did not want to see. He even tried to tell me that it was my duty to go, emphasising that she was my mother after all.

'I pushed his demands to the back of my mind – I just could not bring myself to walk into that house and climb those stairs to her bedroom. A couple of days later, I received a call, telling me she had been rushed to hospital. And still I did not go to her side. I think it was not just my childhood memories of my miserable years in that house that stopped me, but that I could not bear the thought of seeing my mother lying helpless in her bed. I wanted to keep the image in my head of the stern, cold woman she had always been. I did not want my feelings about her confused, if that makes any sense.'

'Yes, it does. But are you saying you did not want to stop hating her, that it was easier for you if you did?'

'I didn't hate her, I never had. That's something I have realised since I have been coming here. I might have loathed a lot of what she did or didn't do, but not her. And in a way I think that was part of my problem. All my life I had wanted her to show me some signs of love. She never had. When she asked for me I wonder if she had wanted to apologise or try and seek my forgiveness. I'll never know now, will I? But even if she had, it would have been too little, too late.'

'Or not, Cassie.'

'Or not, as you say. I suppose I did feel guilty about that. Maybe if my father hadn't said what he did, I might have changed my mind.'

'What was it he said, Cassie?'

'That she had never done anything wrong. Can you imagine that? Talk about him rewriting history! I was waiting for him to say she had been a really good mother, but at least he left it at that. And I so wanted to tell him exactly what it was my mother had done wrong. That, forgetting the lack of love shown towards my brothers and me, she had, although he clearly never faced up to it, been his accomplice in my abuse. For heaven's sake, she knew who had made me pregnant! And what did she do apart from helping me get rid of it? Nothing, she did nothing! And more than that, she had never stopped him taking out his frustration and anger on my brothers. Their treatment of Jimmy was bad enough – but Ben? Between them, with their bullying and mockery, they changed a sweet-natured simple boy into someone quite different. And those pills she gave me so I would abort, were they even safe? Did she even care one way or the other? I hate to think what she might have been capable of, had they not worked. She would have done anything to protect him. Oh yes, I wanted to spit all of that out to my father, all right!'

'But you didn't?'

'No, he sounded, oh I don't know, vulnerable, if that's the right word. And as much as I was tempted, I simply could not bring myself to rip away his delusions. It seemed as though he wanted all the guilt to be his and to see her as someone completely blameless. I suppose we believe what we want to.'

'Yes, that's true of most of us, Cassie. People can be very good at fooling themselves. Now, I know your mother is dead, but is this the time she actually died?'

'Yes, the next phone call I received was from my father telling me she had slipped away during the night. There had only been him sitting beside her bed. Jimmy also had refused to come and Ben would have been better off left at the house. If I had felt pangs of guilt when I had refused to see her, this was nothing to the waves of it I felt when it sank in that she was really dead. God, I felt bad. I tried telling myself that I had nothing to feel guilty about, but I knew I had been cowardly not going to see her.'

'She was still your mother, Cassie. Many people find it difficult to wipe away some feeling for a parent, no matter how bad that parenting has been.'

'Yes, you are right there. That was something I realised then. I wanted to be able to, but I just couldn't. I went to the funeral, not that I wanted to, but I felt I had to. As you say, she was my mother. Anyhow, what could I say to my husband if I hadn't? June was so concerned. She hugged me, asked if there was anything she could do for me. I just told her that if she could look after our boys when John and I went to the funeral, I would be very grateful. They were four and six and I felt they were too young to stand at a graveside. I also hoped June did not notice that I was not at all grief-stricken. Not only was the woman who laid in the morgue my mother, she was also comparatively young, having not even reached her fiftieth birthday. If June did wonder why my eyes were dry, she made no comment.'

Jimmy had refused to go. But then he had told me that once he left that house nothing would bring him back. Not just to the house, but anywhere that meant he might have to see them. He even refused to come to my wedding, so I should have guessed what his reaction would be.

I had rung him as there was still some contact between us, but very little. He was not overfriendly – he never was whenever I tried to keep in contact and that hurt. I couldn't help but think how, when he was small, he had followed me about, and how his face had lit up when I came home from school. But bitterness had scarred him; wiped out his childhood memories of how we had once been close.

'I told you,' he said, 'that I would never want to see either of them again. Not even when they are in boxes and safe from causing more harm to anyone.'

And that was the end of that conversation.

So John and I went together in our car to the crematorium. I had not wanted to sit with my father and Ben in the huge black car that followed slowly behind the hearse. In fact, once there, I did not want to sit near Dad at all, but we had little choice, for not many people had turned up. I felt a rush of something like sorrow when I saw that apart from a couple of neighbours and a few of my father's dodgy car dealer friends, there had been so few people in my mum's life who cared about her. I also felt sad that the children she had given birth to had been forced away by my father's and her indifference. Whatever her faults, it was still a lonely end.

If I felt sorry for that, when my eyes landed on Ben I felt such an overwhelming sense of pity that made me want to cry even more than my mother's death had. He had grown into a big, ungainly man. His face, though, was vacant, his gait still clumsy. But it was he, the one who had been treated so badly, who with tears coursing down his face, let out deep noisy sobs as snot dropped down onto his shirt. He sat next to our father who, when I glanced over at him, suddenly appeared smaller, sort of shrunken somehow. I saw then that he, who was not wont to show emotion, was completely consumed by grief.

That was the first time that I understood that he had actually loved my mother, which made what he had done to me even less comprehensible.

That was the last time I ever saw him too, a man completely broken by his wife's death. I was not surprised to learn that it had not taken long for him to join her. From what I heard, drink destroyed him – I suppose it was cirrhosis. He had not died alone, though: Ben, faithful to the end, was at his side.

And here's the bit that I find saddest: Ben had to be placed in a home. And yes, before you ask, I did visit him, just the once. The home called me as I was down as his next of kin. That big awkward man with haunted eyes kept asking for our parents, as if he had forgotten they were dead. I don't think he even recognised me. I told Jimmy what happened to Ben. He said he hoped his brother was being cared for at last, but he never came.

Ben died within months of our parents. One of the carers at the home told me that he rarely spoke, except to speak their names, and never once smiled during the few months he was there. He just sat in his chair, staring out of the window – he missed them that much. I asked what he had died of.

'A broken heart,' the carer said.

Chapter Twenty-Nine

'Cassie, I still feel there is something you have not told me. All you have said is that after your mother's funeral, you never saw your father again. In fact, it seems that you had broken off contact, not just with him but more or less with your brothers as well. But you have not said what happened to cause that break. So tell me, why did you say that was the last time? You could have decided that when you got married, you were out of the house by then.'

Over the weeks I had been in therapy that was one of the questions I had dreaded being asked and now it was too late to avoid answering my therapist. I had always feared she would bring up this gap in my recollections.

I twisted my bands; snap, they went against my arm, little tingles of pain meant to keep me from staying in my own head with only jumbled thoughts for company. Snap, I went again, fully aware that my therapist was watching me intently.

'Cassie?'

'I should, I know that, have done what Jimmy did; broke off all contact with them. I could have told my husband and June that I did not get on with them; that they had never been supportive parents. The fact that my younger brother refused to come to my wedding if they were going to be there would have made my reasons believable.'

'So why didn't you?'

'I don't know. But if I had, I would not be sitting here now, would I?'

And once that admission was made, for the second time since I had met my therapist, it was impossible to hold back the sobs. She waited until I had calmed a little before she poured out two cups of coffee and passed me one, together with the tissues and the ashtray.

'Here, Cassie, drink this. I think you had better light a cigarette as well. We don't want to waste your session, do we?'

I think it was more her tone of cool common sense that helped me pull myself together. I blew my nose, lit up and took a deep gulp of the strong coffee.

'He used to come round, you know, to my house, when my mother was still alive and my husband was out. I know I should not even have opened the door to him or at least told him to go away, but he still had some power over me, and I hated myself for that.

It must have been around three years after my wedding that I first saw him coming up the path. When he knocked on the door I sat trembling in my sitting room, telling my children to hush. I did not want him inside my home. Certainly not when he was alone and my husband was not around. I thought if I just sat there, very quietly, he would go away. He knew I was there, though. When he pressed his face to the window I could see him so clearly looking through it, just staring at me. Sick with panic, I just didn't know what to do. I wanted to shout go away but the children knew he was their grandfather.

'It's only your dad,' he shouted. 'Come on, girl, open the door,' and what could I do? The children, sensing my panic, were beginning to look frightened. Plus any moment a neighbour might see him and wonder what was going on. So I went into the hall and opened the door. And that is when I should have said calmly, as an adult should, for him to go away.'

'Do you think he would have?' my therapist wanted to know.

'Yes, if he had seen that all his power over me had gone then he would, I am sure, have turned around and walked away. But of course, I was my usual pathetic weak self. Instead of behaving like an adult, I regressed to being the child who would obey him, no matter how much I did not want to. I stood aside and allowed him to come in. On that visit he worked very hard at not just being the nice father but the nice grandfather as well. Sweets were produced for the children, friendly conversation was directed at me. He admired how we had done up the house, which we had decorated in light colours: blues, cream and yellow. I had wanted it to look as different from my parents' one as possible. I couldn't help being pleased by the compliment and muttered thanks. He asked to hold his smallest grandson, a request I reluctantly said yes to.

'Hints were dropped about being thirsty and before I knew it there I was in the kitchen making tea. Of course I asked myself what the hell I was doing, but that didn't stop me. An hour passed before, with a glance at the clock, he said how time had flown and he had better get a move on.'

'And he came back?'

'Oh, yes. After that first visit he began to drop in occasionally. Never put a foot wrong, I have to say that for him. No snide comments, no finding an excuse to touch me, not even sideways glances coming in my direction. In other words, there was nothing to make me feel wary or uncomfortable. Gradually I began to relax at him coming round. He would bring round little gifts for the boys and sometimes a bunch of flowers or a box of chocolates for me. He always told me that they were from Mum as well, but I really doubt if she had any knowledge of his visits.

'I began to believe that the nice father had returned. The one I had often believed he was when I was a little girl. I suppose I had never stopped wanting that sense of normality in my life. Or rather, being part of a normal family.

'You know when your friends are bringing up happy memories of their childhood or get out the photo albums that show smiling parents and their children? I wanted to be able to do that too. I suppose that was the reason I was stupid enough to fall for his nice father, nice grandfather act.'

My voice dried up then; I found myself looking at my therapist helplessly.

'He did not stay like that, did he, Cassie?'

I froze for a second. 'She knows,' I thought, with some degree of certainty. 'She knows what happened, she is just waiting for me to tell her.'

'No,' I answered softly, 'he didn't. It took over a year before he showed that the nice father was just a figment of my imagination. The last day I ever saw my father on my own was on a chilly winter's morning.'

I took a deep breath then and allowed my mind to slip back to that very last time my father and I had been alone together.

'It had begun like any other weekday. Paul, my eldest, had started infants school, so wrapping both boys up snugly, we made the short journey to the school. It had snowed during the night and above us the swollen grey clouds promised more. The few trees on the estate were cloaked in silver, ice crystals crunched beneath our feet while our wispy, vaporised breath swirled around our heads. The crispness of the morning cleared my mind and made me feel quite full of energy. When Ken and I got back to the house I made a steaming mug of hot chocolate for me and a milky one for him. "We'll drink that and go outside, build a snowman," I told him and received a wide gappy smile in response, a promise that never materialised.

'I had hardly finished my drink when a knock on the door announced my father's arrival. He was holding a purple elephant in his arms and I laughed at the incongruous sight of a dark-haired man in work clothes, carrying a child's toy. Another beaming smile spread over Ken's face when he saw his present and his chubby little arms rose to take it.

'There was no thought in my head then that this visit to my house was to be a very different one. The faint whiff of alcohol should have warned me, but it was not until he said, "You know, Cassie, you are still my special girl," that a mixture of fear and anger sent the icy shivers of memorised fear down my spine. Suddenly all I could see were his hands with their fine black hairs, the spiders that had frightened me so much as a child. "No," I said to myself and raising my eyes to meet his, I recognised the expression on his face.

'I wanted to scream, to tell him to leave, but I was paralysed. Not just my body, my vocal cords were also refusing to work.

'He moved then – I would never have thought that a man of his age could be so swift. I was still nervously holding the remains of my cup of chocolate, I had not even had the time to put it down. It was he who jerked it from my hand and placed it on the coffee table.

'"Don't want that spilt all over your nice new carpet, do we, Cassie? Now, tell me, have you been missing your old man then?"

'I shook my head wildly.

'"I don't believe you, Cassie. Girls always remember their first."

'His hands snaked up my skirt; they went under me, pulling me forward until I was half on, half off the chair. I tried to push him away, but he was too heavy. He laughed at my futile efforts, making my fear turn to rage and I spat at him.

'"That was not very nice, Cassie," he said and laughed mockingly at me as he wiped the spittle from his chin.

'"Ken ..." I said and this time my voice was pleading.

'"He's happy with his elephant. Not taking any notice of us, is he?" was his answer but I knew my son was watching and it would not take long before the atmosphere in the room would either make him come to me or start crying.

'"I think upstairs then, Cassie, as you don't want your son to watch you having a good time."

'I begged him then: "Please," I said, "don't, please. I'm married now, I have children."

'"And have you told your husband about you and me, Cassie?"

'My silence answered him.

'"Then you won't be telling him about this time either. You have 30 seconds. Either I rip your clothes off down here or you go upstairs and take them off."

'What choice did I have?' I asked my therapist desperately, when I got to that part of my story. 'How could I scream out in the hope my neighbours would come? Not when the man in my sitting room was my own father. And I knew it would be impossible to make a run for it – he was too fast and too strong. Ken started whimpering then, he had realised something was wrong. I told him I was just going upstairs. My legs were shaking so much that I don't know how I got up them. And then that bastard raped me, not in the bedroom but right there on the landing. Pulled my skirt up, tore down my knickers and once again I heard the sound that had always

305

brought my arms out in goosebumps: his zip being undone. And do you know what was even worse than him invading my body? The sound of my little boy's wails; he knew all right that something bad was happening.'

As I told my therapist about that afternoon the tears threatened again.

'I changed after that,' I told her.

'Cassie, that is hardly surprising now, is it? You have to accept that you suffered a terrible ordeal. You should have had counselling then. You must see that and stop blaming yourself. What happened after that?'

'Nothing. I bought a heavy chain for the front door, but I need not have bothered – he never tried to come round again. I told my husband that I did not want my parents invited to our house or June's. I said that my father had come round the worse for drink and frightened Ken. That was enough for him to agree.

'He did ring just once, blamed the drink. I hung up. The next time he called was when my mother was dying.'

Chapter Thirty

'Cassie, from what you have told me you were both a good mother and a contented wife up until when your father assaulted you. You said it changed you. Can you just try and tell me in what way that was?'

'I might never have enjoyed sex. I really did hate the feel of a naked body against mine, not to mention the stickiness and the smell, but I had known that to stay in a marriage, it was expected of me. Luckily my husband was not very experienced. Well, not with girls who were considered to be nice ones. And when we met that was the sort of girl he believed me to be. So my not being very passionate might have been noticed, but he did not seem to consider it abnormal. No doubt other men told him that not all women want to "make love", as my husband called it, more than once a week. And once a week I was able to manage it. And I did love him; he was kind, he made me feel cared for. So I wanted to please him.

'And although I did not enjoy the sex bit, I did like the affection he gave me. You know, cuddling up on the settee once the kids were in bed and hugs when I had cooked him one of his favourite meals. In fact, he was a man who was pretty easy to please. But as I said, I changed after my father had assaulted me. I just could not bear to be touched; little lies were invented. I was having heavy periods that had caused anaemia and yes, I told him, I had been to the doctor. He had prescribed some pills. I also added that I was having bad headaches. In other words, I was using any excuse I could imagine to sleep with my back turned to my husband. I ignored his concern, for to begin with he believed me. It was when I started spurning his affectionate gestures, shrugging off an arm laid affectionately on my shoulder and moving my head to avoid a goodbye kiss that he stopped.'

'What was your husband's response to your actions then?'

'He was hurt, of course he was. That made me feel guilty and then I was angry that he had made me feel that way. His mother sensed something was wrong although somehow I doubt if she knew what it was, he wouldn't have told her. Well, boys then didn't talk to their mothers about such things. She asked me more than once if everything was all right.'

'And what was your answer?'

'I repeated some of the lies I had told my husband and assured her that I had been to the doctor. But it was not only my husband's embraces I avoided, but those from friends as well. Even worse, I found it hard to show my sons any normal affection. I no longer wanted them sitting on my knee or running up to me with their arms spread to receive a hug. I know they were little boys, but I began to feel that their demands were draining the life out of me. I started to imagine the men they would grow into. Had their grandfather passed down his genes? Would they grow to be like him? Would they turn into sexual predators?'

Those were the thoughts that spun ceaselessly in my mind until the headaches I had pretended to have became real.

That was the beginning of me feeling completely isolated.

They say time heals, but in my case my jumbled-up brain just got worse. My life was falling apart and my children suffered because of it.

'You know what I think is so awful?' I said to my therapist.

'No, Cassie, tell me.'

'When I gave birth and the nurse placed them in my arms, I promised each of them that I would not be like my mother. They were going to grow up in a happy home. John and I would make sure that they always felt loved and secure. But in the end, I let them down, didn't I?'

'You were not well, Cassie. The social worker did not see a bad mother, she saw one who was having a breakdown. That is why she arranged for you to see me. You might not remember what you told her, but let's say it was enough for her to be concerned. You have to start being a little kinder to yourself.

'Now, at our next session I want to work through what finally sent you over the edge. Or to put it in layman's language, what was the straw that broke the camel's back?'

I felt like hugging her then. Her words had at least taken some of my guilt away.

*

For so long I had been convinced that there were people who knew my secret. I saw the way they looked at me when I went to the shops; I heard mutters, saw at first pity and then something else, fleetingly, not fear exactly, but a desire to avoid me.

No longer did my sons play with the other children and bring them into the house. And I knew without asking why that was.

Not because I smelt of drink, not because my hygiene was slipping, not because my children were beginning to look neglected. No, none of those things, but I knew it was because they knew about my father.

That was the belief I had, and as the days passed, it only grew stronger.

I was drunk the day I was reported to social services. I had forgotten my husband had told me he was working late. The children would be all right being left for a while, I told myself, as I walked determinedly to the off-licence.

Chapter Thirty-One

I did not need my therapist to ask the usual opening question. I felt, after all these months, that I was finally ready to talk about the part of my story that I was most ashamed about. I took a deep breath and started the session.

'My downfall, if we are to call it that, happened because I made one very bad mistake.'

'What was it, Cassie, your mistake?'

'I confided in the wrong person and that was when my world fell apart. Nina, she was called, and I thought she was a close friend when I shared my secret with her.'

'How long had you known her?'

'Oh, a while, since our kids were small. She had a bit of a reputation, but I did not take much notice of what I heard. She was always nice to me. When our kids played together she and I would sit and natter while we drank copious cups of tea. I just put the gossip about her down to her having three kids and no husband. Well, to be honest maybe the bleached blonde hair and heavy make-up didn't help either. She had told everyone that her husband had left her and I believed her, even if others didn't. I've got my doubts now though.

'Anyhow, it was Nina's suggestion, when she thought I was a bit depressed, that we went out together one evening. "You need to get out of the house more," she had said, "a good night out would cheer you up," she had added, and after a bit of persuasion I said, "Yes, all right. Can't do any harm, can it?"

'When I told my husband he said it was a good idea to get away from the kids for a bit and that he was pleased I had made a friend on the estate. And he was more than happy to take care of the children while I had a "bit of well-deserved fun". Those were his words, not mine. That was the sort of man he was back then. Some sixth sense told me to arrange to meet Nina at her house and not have her call round for me. Just as well, I thought when I saw how she had dressed for a night out at a pub! I was a bit embarrassed by her then to be truthful. She really had done the mutton dressed as lamb bit far too much: a very short skirt and a strappy top that was much too revealing. Can't remember what I wore, but certainly nothing like that. If I disapproved of how she was dressed, she was not so enthusiastic about my appearance either. She made me put on a bit more make-up and sprayed me with some perfume that I thought smelt a bit sweet before we left. Then, looking me up and down, she said, "With those long legs of yours, you could look a right smasher, Cassie, if you just wore something a little tighter." I felt flattered, of course I did, even though I wanted to say that my husband liked me just the way I was. But I thought better of it.

'The pub we went to was not one I had been in before. "My local," she told me with a wink as we walked through the doors into a thick haze of cigarette smoke. She certainly was well known there. We hardly had to open our handbags because of the free drinks bought for us. Men just flocked around her, though half the time, with the loud music coming from the jukebox, I could hardly hear what they were saying. I suppose the night was fun and she must have enjoyed it, because she asked me to go out with her again. Though she did tease me, but not unkindly, about the way I dressed. "If you've got it, flaunt it" was certainly her motto.

'I used the excuse that I could hardly leave the house dressed to the nines and tell my husband that I was just having a drink with a friend, could I? Anyhow, I did not have anything glitzy in my wardrobe.'

'So what made you tell her, as you call it, "your secret"?'

'I suppose everything was just getting too much for me. I still don't know what good I thought it would do. But then thinking was not my strong point at that time in my life,' I added dryly.

'I wanted, I don't know, a shoulder to cry on, or someone who had a magic wand they could wave over my head and make all my problems disappear. I thought she would have been sympathetic, and OK, there was too much drink involved, but still ... Anyhow, I told her, told her what my father had done to me as child, even how I had become pregnant and that he would still not leave me alone.'

'And what was her reaction?'

'It was just horrible. She called me a pervert. Said if I was still speaking to my father, then not to tell her I had been an innocent. That if he had really forced me, as I wanted her to believe, then why had I not asked for help? No, it was my mother she felt sorry for, not me.

'I left her house in floods of tears. She was the one friend I thought I had and now she despised me. That was not the worst though. Next thing I knew she told her kids they could not play with mine any more. And then she told other people on the estate. God knows what was said, but I was aware of the judgemental looks that came my way.'

'Was that when your heavy drinking started?'

'I suppose the beginning of my drinking really began when I went to the pub with Nina. Even before that in fact, when I had the odd glass or two at her house. It did not take long for me to find that it was the second glass that made my problems blur a bit. So no, I had already started before I told her.'

'And when you stopped going to Nina's house?'

'That was when it started getting out of control. To begin with it was just a bottle of cheap wine from the supermarket that I would sip at throughout the day. It took a while for my husband to notice. By the time he did, I had found the litre-sized bottles and by then not only did I find it impossible to stop, I didn't want to. I started going to the park, sitting there drowning my sorrows, before staggering home. I found myself even going out in the evenings to buy some more. The neighbours, hearing that I was a drunk neglectful mother as well as whatever Nina had told them I was, turned their backs on me but not their eyes. Every move I made was watched. My visits to the off-licence and the resulting escape into oblivion, was noted. Gossip was rife and feeling their contempt, I drank more.

'To this day I do not know which of my neighbours made the call to social services. Though I might still blame them for their condemnation, I can hardly blame them for that. I accept that I should not have allowed my neighbours' chatter about me to send me over the edge. Tackled them maybe, or just kept myself to myself. Not let those looks that bore into my back as I passed get to me. Or give in to that inner voice telling me a drink would make me feel better.

'It was terribly wrong of me to have left my children in the house alone while I sat in the park feeling sorry for myself. Nor should I have staggered back home drunk and tearful in full view of the entire neighbourhood. Even worse, it was also in full view of the two social workers who had been called out and were waiting on my doorstep.

'Oh, they were kind; kinder than I deserved. But nothing was going to stop them leaving with the children. The police, who had been called, also explained that they were being removed for their safety. My husband, who had rushed home from work after the unpleasant phone call he had received, after pleading with the police and social services, reluctantly accepted that he had to agree to them going. He was the breadwinner, so he could not stay at home and look after them.

'What I remember most about that terrible day was my children being led away. I was hugging them and they, not understanding what was happening, were crying. One social worker stayed behind while the others drove off with the children. I will never forget watching their worried faces looking back at John and me through the car's rear window. My husband sat there, refusing to look at me, as he admitted he knew about my drinking, but not that I was leaving the children alone in the house. And yes, he told them, he had pleaded with me to stop.

'They asked about his mother, if she could help. His reply was that she would not be able to cope. They did not ask about my parents – I suppose some of the gossip whispered on the local grapevine had been shared with them.

'And whispers, I have found, carry further than shouts.'

Chapter Thirty-Two

'I have a lot to thank social services for, I know that,' I said to my therapist, before pulling out the memories of the day. I finally knew I had hit rock bottom and started describing it to her.

'My husband left almost at the same time as the children. Packed a bag and with hardly a word passing his lips, he walked out. I just sat there, hardly moving, with tears running unchecked down my cheeks while the house gradually emptied. Then there was only Margaret, one of the social workers, remaining. I can't remember what it was I had told her, I'm sure it was a jumbled-up version of my life. I know that I asked if she had heard the gossip about me. She was careful with her answer, but it was clear, by some of the questions she asked, that she had been told something about my father and me.

'She made me tea – I do remember that – and also that she kept reassuring me that there was help available, and she was going to make sure I got it. She told me more than once that my sons were only going into care until I felt able to look after them. I understood though that social services would have to be certain that I was capable of looking after them properly before they would consider returning them to my care.

'Margaret asked if there was anyone I could call, someone who could stay with me. A question meant kindly, but one that reduced me to more tears. It just emphasised to me how alone I was. Hearing, amidst my sobs, that there wasn't, she promised that she would be back. That I was not going to have to deal with everything alone. Hearing no response, she leant down and took my hand. "Cassie," she said, "are you listening?"

'I was; I just felt too dazed to talk any more.

'"I'm going to come back in the morning. Everything will work out in the end, even though it's hard to believe that now," she told me.

'She did ask if there was any alcohol in the house. There wasn't, I told her. Then she made me promise to go straight to bed.

'"Sleep it off, Cassie. Things will look better in the morning. I'll be round quite early, and we'll talk more then."'

'I hardly thought that anything was going to be better when I woke, but I did as she told me – I was too worn out not to. Plus, I was not going to set one foot outside the house and face the neighbours. To my relief, she kept her promise. At ten o'clock I heard a knock on the door and let her in.

'We did talk more. I told her some of the details about the abuse. Not the rape though; that I was too ashamed of. More cups of tea were drunk as she listened carefully.

'"I thought as much, from what you told me last night, Cassie. I was right too in what I said to you then: this is not something you can deal with on your own. Do you remember me telling you that I would make sure you got help?"

'"Yes," I replied, not adding that at the time I had little faith in her promises.

'It was then that she opened her bag and passed me the cream card, the one with the time of my first appointment here written on it.

'"I've spoken to her, and she's managed to fit you in tomorrow morning. She's good, Cassie, she will help you. I've also arranged for you to see your children. I'm going to come and take you to them tomorrow afternoon."

'"What have they been told?" I asked nervously, thinking of how frightened they had looked the day before.

'"That you are not very well. So the nice people they are staying with are looking after them until you are better. And that is all Paul's school knows as well."

'"The people they are staying with must think I am a terrible mother," I said, as more tears welled up.

'"No, Cassie, just someone having problems, that's all."

'And that,' I said with a smile to my therapist, 'is how I came to meet you, isn't it?'

'Yes, it's been a long and painful journey for you. Now tell me, what have you thought we have been working towards?'

'To come to terms with my childhood and stop burying all the good memories under the bad ones.'

'Yes, I'm going to tell you, not a story exactly, but about a charity I came across when I did some work in South Africa. In the overcrowded townships, where the gangs rule with guns and drugs, childhood ends before it has really begun, young boys believe that to become a man they must join them. After their initiation, they receive the first of the tattoos that tells the world which gang they are a member of.

'But there are some, who once they reach adulthood, or when they come out of prison, want to leave that life of crime, brutality and violence that they had been made to believe was their destiny. They know that to escape the future, which has been marked out for them, those tattoos have to be erased; a procedure that until recently was far too costly for them to afford. That changed when a group of young artists heard of their predicament. They, along with skilled tattooists, use their combined skills to transform menacing tattoos into flowers, birds and butterflies. Those young men can look at those images with pride and smile as they dream of a new future. For now the ugliness is hidden under beauty.

'Isn't that what many of us wish to do with our past? So, Cassie, make the good memories become the overlay that hides all the bad ones.'

And finally, I understood fully what it was she had been asking of me.

'So that's why you kept talking about my good memories,' I said.

'Yes. And now, we are going to talk about your sons and your visits to them.'

Chapter Thirty-Three

So I made my mind travel back to just a few weeks earlier, although sitting in my therapist's office, it felt much longer. She was right, it had been a journey, one that was gradually changing me into a woman I could begin to feel some respect for.

'My first visit to my sons was almost more than I could bear. I was introduced to the woman who was caring for them. Janice, a short rather pump brunette about ten years older than me, took my hand and led me into the room where they were playing with a box of Lego. Two little faces stared up at me, then their mouths stretched into smiles before in unison, they both yelled, "Mummy!" I wanted to kneel down on the floor, wrap my arms around them, breathe in their small boy smell of soap and talcum powder, and whisper in their ears that I loved them. That was what I wanted to do, but I did none of that.

'Instead, self-consciously, I sat on one of the low comfy chairs where, almost as though I was speaking to children I did not know, I found only stilted questions coming out of my mouth. It was my youngest son, Ken, who broke the ice.

He had drawn a picture he wanted me to have. "For you, Mummy," he said, as he came to my side. I smiled a little then. As I had once drawn a square house, so had he, but instead of placing a tree beside it, he had drawn a family of four: two adults, one in trousers, one in a skirt, and two smaller figures.

"'It's lovely," I managed to say, "I'm going to pin it up in the kitchen so I can see it every day."

"'I want to go home, Mummy," he said, leaning against my knee, and I whispered, "Soon."

'Seeing Ken receiving my attention, Paul decided he too wanted some.

"'Mummy, I need to pee," he said and as I half-rose from my seat with my hand already beginning to stretch out to take his, Janice sprang up.

"'I'll take you Paul, and Ken, you had better come too. We don't want to be jumping up and down all afternoon."

'I understood then that I had not won enough gold stars to be allowed to be on my own with my children.

'The hour I had with them finished too soon, but in another way it lasted too long. I knew my boys did not really understand why they were living in a stranger's house. Also, I was aware the whole time I was there that every move I made and every move I didn't was being noted. Margaret had, since I met her, proved she had my interests at heart, but she was also part of a team who would ultimately decide on my children's fate.

'After the first few visits, where Janice always made me feel most welcome, I began to find them easier, and after a month, I did what I had wanted to do at that first meeting, but still couldn't bring myself to do. I knelt on the floor, and confident that my sessions with you were already working, I reached out and hugged them.'

My therapist smiled at me when I got to that part of my story. 'As I said, Cassie, it has been a journey. I know it's one that has not been easy for you. It is very common for people who have been abused as children to fear intimacy, even with their own children.'

'I just want my children back home,' I blurted out.

'I know you do,' was her answer.

Not long after that I had another visit from social services. They had talked to my husband. John was no longer angry, but still very upset. He needed more time before he met with me to discuss the future. He admitted he had heard some of the gossip. What had happened to me was outside of his understanding. He simply could not comprehend why I had not confided in him or how I had stayed in touch with my parents after I was married. Not only that, I had invited them to our wedding.

He would not contest the children being placed back with me, as long as he was convinced that I was capable of being a good mother. And of course he would want visiting rights, but just not yet.

It had been decided that moving the children back to an estate where people knew about me was not a good idea. Not for them, and not for my mental health either. When I heard that, for a moment I believed I had lost them for good.

But no, a house on another estate had been found, if I was agreeable to moving there.

'It will be a new start,' they said. 'No one will know anything about you there.'

'And my children?'

'Once you are settled in,' Margaret told me, 'they will be able to come home.'

Of course, my story did not end there. I was in therapy for well over two years. And as my therapist had told me, I found there is no magic cure for overcoming my early life. What I learnt though was to accept it; rid myself of the anger and resentment; to take responsibility for some of the mistakes I had made and stop blaming my past for all of them.

My husband came to several of the sessions. However, we both accepted that our marriage was irreparable. For our sons' sakes we made our parting amicable and over the years we have become good friends.

Once my sons were both in the junior school, I talked again to Margaret. I told her I wanted to work with the elderly.

'Because of your grandmother?' she asked.

Maybe she was right, not that it matters. I have found a vocation that gives me satisfaction. Where yes, I can put my arms around frail shoulders, hold wrinkled hands and smile into the eyes of the confused and give them reassurance.

I can truly say that I have found peace.

My sons are now grown men, with families of their own.

I can hug them now.

Acknowledgements

I dedicate this book to my very good friends who have helped me come from the dark into the light, including Maria, Sophie and Jane for all your support helping me to become who I am today. My deepest gratitude to my family – I couldn't have done it without your support; and a big thank you to my work colleagues – you all know who you are. Not forgetting Toni for all her hard work and helping me to achieve my goal. Thank you all for being part of my journey. I love you all.

Toni Maguire

One woman who found the courage to share her story inspired others to find their voice

Toni Maguire has published two bestselling books which covered her own story of her childhood abuse and finding a way of moving on from her past, *Don't Tell Mummy* and *When Daddy Comes Home*. Her success encouraged others who had kept their childhood secrets hidden to approach her and share their stories. She has so far co-written six memoirs and sold over 1.5 million books worldwide. To find out more about Toni and her story visit www.tonimaguire.co.uk

Also from Toni Maguire:

They Stole My Innocence

The shocking true story of a young girl abused in one of the most notorious care homes

Five-year-old Madeleine was living a daily nightmare. In a dark, grey building in Jersey, she was just another orphan, defenceless and alone. Unbeknownst to the outside world, the care home manager was using her like she was his toy. And, worse still, the home was selling the children to men who would inflict on them the worst possible abuse.

This is Madeleine's heart-breaking story and her fight to survive.

ISBN 9781785033513

Order direct from www.penguin.co.uk

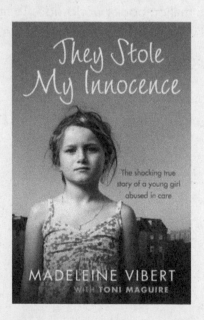